Paw Prints in the Sand

Elizabeth Parker

First Edition

ISBN-13: 978-1477575659

ISBN-10: 1477575650

To order this book or any book written by Elizabeth Parker, or if you have any questions or comments, please visit me at www.elizabethparkerbooks.com.

A portion of the proceeds from the sales of this book will be donated to an animal rescue group.

To Buddy Senior Thank you for showing us the true meaning of love without reservation. You'll never be forgotten.

To my husband-I know every time you walk in the house, you look around to see if another dog is living with us. Thanks for opening our home and your heart to so many of them!

To my pups- I'm glad that you rescued us and changed our lives for the better.

To my mom who has put up with me adopting dogs before I even knew how to speak. Thank you.

To all of the unfortunate dogs that have suffered in any way, just know that you are loved by those who haven't even met you.

To Rascal-the lone duck toller who happened to coincidentally come along and tear at my own heartstrings as I was completing this book. I pray that you are happy, safe and loved beyond belief in your new home.

Prologue: Precious Innocence

A dog is not a thing. A thing is replaceable. A dog is not. A thing is disposable. A dog is not. A thing doesn't have a heart. A dog's heart is bigger than any "thing" you can ever own.

The buildings are always the same; old rusty cages, the unmistakable smell of fear; desperate dogs begging for loving homes, their raspy cries echoing throughout the lonely and frigid hallways.

As you trudge up and down the aisles of a kill shelter, you see that each crate houses an abandoned animal whose yearning eyes plead while your heart melts into a roaring sea of helplessness. How did they get here? Why them? No one deserves this.

You want so badly to rescue them. You'd love to take all of them home, but of course, it isn't feasible.

As you look into the innocent eyes of each dog, you know it'll be less than a week before the older ones lose their life, and the young "vicious" dogs, as they have been stereotypically labeled, only have a few more days at most.

While you're there, you can't help but wonder, do they know? Is there any possible way the dogs realize what cruelty fate has in store for them? Admitting that painful truth to yourself is harder than you ever imagined.

The thought races out of your mind as quickly as it had entered. Not because you don't care—God knows you care more than anything—but because it is too difficult to accept the harsh reality.

But, alas, there's still that somewhat gratifying feeling of knowing that you are there to make a difference in at least one of their lives.

You have a spot, or maybe even two, in your home and more than enough love in your heart to accommodate these precious creatures and hopefully free up some room for another unfortunate stray at the facility in the process.

At least that's how it happened for Chelsea and Anthony Shelton.

Chapter 1: Love Unguarded

There will always be detours in the fascinating game called life. Find the path to your heart's desires, and stay on course.

Chelsea and Anthony had been teenage sweethearts, who, like most at that young age, broke up for a short while to sow their oats before realizing they were true soul mates.

Before they got back together, they each dabbled in the party scene and enjoyed a few drinking binges, complete with the dreaded hangovers the next day, but realized that wasn't the permanent lifestyle they sought after. Eventually, they found their way back into each other's hearts in their early twenties and had been together ever since.

Both became successful, conscientious individuals and though they occasionally had arguments like every married couple, they respected and genuinely cared for one another.

They weren't considered glamorous by any means, but were definitely average in looks. Chelsea had long, brown hair and light green eyes and Anthony was blessed with a muscular physique and full head of thick, sandy brown hair.

Married only four years, they'd already experienced their share of hardships with trying to start their family. They wanted nothing more than to have a child of their own, but after they both underwent a series of medical tests, the doctors revealed that it just wasn't in the cards for them. A major disappointment as since the day they were married, they'd always imagined sharing their lives with at least two children, and a family dog to complete the picture.

With the support of their beloved family and friends, they got over the initial shock of their misfortune, and moved forward with plans to adopt a child. The downside was that according to the adoption agency, it might take years. And there were no guarantees.

Although they were understandably disappointed, they decided that in the interim they would still consummate the second portion of their plan. After giving it some thought, there was no valid reason to put their lives on hold.

They'd been prepared to rescue a shelter dog and each time they sat through the tear-jerking commercials on the television, they realized in their heart that now was as good a time as any.

It was an early Saturday morning when they drove down to the town shelter. The building itself rested at the end of a cul-de-sac, surrounded by nothing but trees and a broken-up parking lot to match the brokenhearted pups inside.

When they ambled in through the double-glass doors, the middle-age volunteer greeted them with a personality as lively as a crumbled piece of that parking lot. Barely acknowledging their arrival, she merely pointed the way toward the gray, metal door that housed the dogs. Then she buried her face in her fitness magazine.

This establishment was known as a kill-shelter, and Chelsea speculated that to volunteer in the facility, it was probably better off that one didn't show any emotion, as demonstrated by the detached woman occupying the front desk.

With so many dogs being neglected, abandoned, dumped, abused, and everything in between, there are never enough facilities to provide shelter for all of them. What adds to the devastation is that often shelter dogs fail to get adopted due to their seemingly aggressive behavior, even if they were once friendly on the outside.

Nine times out of ten, something changes their disposition once they get locked up. Their personalities shift, whether it be from the fear, the isolation, the confusion, the cold cement floors, or the lack of toys. Or it may be from being bereft of exercise, deprived of love, or simply because they can smell the death of their canine peers from the euthanasia rooms. The necessity to survive causes them to lose their trust and more importantly, their confidence.

The unfamiliar noises and lonely environment do nothing to mollify their fears. Since they appear aggressive, the likeliness of them finding a good home diminishes. It's the same doleful story in every facility, yet their population continues to increase daily.

As the door slammed behind Chelsea and Anthony, it resonated, setting off a chorus of frenzied barks from the distressed occupants. The couple walked gingerly past the countless rows of crates, trying their best not to frighten any of the dogs, each one looking more desperate than the last.

Had it not been for one dog's demanding howl, Chelsea might have run out of the building empty handed. The absolute realization and heartache was too much for her to bear.

But that howl.

It was the single thing that caused her to laugh when she was on the verge of tears. That demanding howl, combined with the act of the dog maneuvering his scrawny paw through the cage in a sincere effort to grab her leg, as if to say, "Hey, get over here. Come be my new mom."

Aside from his disheveled exterior, he was indubitably striking. Like most shelter dogs, he was in dire need of a thorough grooming, as his knotted hair was course and his skin flaky. The hardened goop under his eyes appeared as if it hadn't ever been cleaned.

Underneath that tangle of golden fur was a bright-eyed, energetic sweetheart of a dog. His fox-like ears bent forward toward his light brown eyes, which revealed an expression that couldn't be mistaken for anything but hope.

His sparkling personality shined through like an illuminating star, and those same hopeful eyes translated a heartfelt story that words would never be able to accurately describe.

In the cage directly across from him sat a more demure canine that appeared to be his twin. She wasn't nearly as vocal, but just as stunning, if not more so. Her golden fur was also knotted right behind the ears, and her paws were caked with mud, presumably from yesterday's rainfall. She sat erect, the previously white tuft on her chest now gray and soiled. Both of the dogs had clearly been neglected even before they had arrived at the shelter.

Chelsea had already made up her mind when she turned back to catch Anthony's eyes, who was grinning from ear to ear. He didn't have to say a word.

"Both?" she whispered, knowing her husband well enough to read his mind.

He nodded. "Absolutely." Though he was a man broad in stature, he was normally not flagrant with his emotions. This time, however, tears pooled in the corners of his hazel eyes. Apparently, the dismal environment was heart wrenching for him as well.

While they discussed it, another volunteer turned the corner and greeted them. This one seemed to have notably more compassion than the woman occupying the front desk. She smiled warmly at them before realizing that they were interested.

"Have you decided on which dog you'd like to take home today?" she asked Chelsea. After helping out at the shelter for so many years, it was easy for the volunteer to recognize the vibrant sparkle in Chelsea's eyes that could signify only love at first sight—the special kind that often transpires between human and dog.

Chelsea couldn't wait for Anthony to speak, so she took the lead. "Yes, please. We're interested in these two." She pointed to the female and male. The male was ignoring the conversation, focusing on reaching through the bars, trying to grasp the shoelaces on Chelsea's sneaker.

They asked the volunteer a number of questions, including whether or not the dogs were related, wondering if perhaps they were brother and sister. The volunteer said that, to the best of her knowledge, they were not.

She informed them that they had been surrendered within two days of each other. The male's age was estimated to be approximately a year and a half, while the female was about a year old.

Both were unmistakably purebred Nova Scotia duck tolling retrievers. They had all the markings, the white tuft, the fox-like ears, the pink nose and lips, and the light eyes that matched their golden coat.

While some families have no other choice but to surrender their dogs because of hardships, financial difficulty or medical issues, these dogs were given up needlessly.

Apparently, the male was given up because he barked incessantly, and his owners couldn't handle the atrocious noise level. They admitted that they didn't have the time or the patience to train him.

The female was turned in because she wasn't housebroken yet, even though that was due to no fault of her own. Rather than train her, the previous owners argued that dogs should instinctively know how to take care of business. They voiced their frustration and said they wanted her out of the house as soon as possible. The shelter took her in that same day.

Hearing their heartbreaking stories further confirmed their decision, and it took only moments for Chelsea and Anthony to fill out the necessary paperwork.

Within an hour, the dogs were on their way to their new home, finally given a second chance at enjoying their lives as they should, which was an opportunity many other dogs are never granted.

Sadly, the pair was hesitant to meander out of the facility. Both dogs tucked their tails between their legs, both were frightened and shy—most likely stemming from their stay at the shelter.

But once they walked outside with their new owners, the warm breeze wafted a plethora of new scents to their keen noses, allowing them to do what came naturally to them—just be dogs. To a dog, smelling the scents of other dogs, humans, or creatures that had visited a path before them is a luxury in itself.

Hearing the natural songs of the wildlife, even smelling something simple such as flowers that are in bloom, is a wondrous joy. To them, each unique scent tells a captivating story and is a vibrant indication that they are still alive, and more importantly, it signifies that there is hope.

Before long, the two dogs slowly began to wag their tails with unbridled enthusiasm. Moments later, they even danced around each other, demonstrating the customary canine greeting that initiates a friendship and builds the foundation for an everlasting relationship. It was a sight to remember.

Before leaving the shelter, Chelsea and Anthony had been advised that the female had been spayed, but the male had not yet been altered. So the first thing they did once the adoption was finalized was make an appointment at the vet to have Spice neutered. The appointment was set for the first of March, three weeks after his adoption date. Sugar wouldn't have to go to the vet for shots until a month later.

Chapter 2: Bundled Surprises

Love knows no bounds, especially between dogs. If every canine was spayed and neutered, the volume of those suffering would be greatly reduced.

The next few weeks proved to be pleasantly constructive as well as a lot of work for the proud new parents of Sugar and Spice. With any new dog that's adopted into a household, it's common to go through the familiarizing stage, which simply means the new owners have to learn their dog's habits, fears, and quirks.

Similarly, Sugar and Spice learned to adapt to their new owners as well as their new lives, even though it was far better than their perplexing stay at the shelter.

Naturally, both dogs were unsure of themselves, as many rescued dogs are. It comes with the territory. At one point in their young lives, both dogs had families and felt secure. It's impossible for them to understand the transitions they had endured, and it's safe to say that life at the shelter was a very distressing experience for them.

In their new surroundings, they were given a loving environment, the kind of environment that all dogs should be fortunate enough to have, including a warm bed, an abundance of toys and companionship with both each other and their human parents. They were slowly coming around, but it still took a while before they were fully acclimated.

With so much mayhem having crashed down on their lives, one thing was certain. Each relied heavily on the other, and they rarely spent time apart. Wherever Sugar went, Spice was sure to follow. Chelsea often took solace in watching the two of them sleep nestled together on their new, plush dog beds. They quickly became the best of friends and had formed their own pack.

When they brought Sugar in for her vaccinations, the veterinarian greeted them and welcomed them inside. She was a likable, warm, and compassionate woman. This was the second time they had been to her office, as the first was to get Spice neutered a few weeks back.

She took the time to examine Sugar and then stood up to speak to the owners. She wasn't sure how they'd take the news, but decided to convey it in a positive manner. Like oblivious parents in shock, the couple could only offer a blank stare when the veterinarian said that congratulations were in order. "There are multiple heartbeats. Sugar's pregnant!"

"I'm sorry. I'm certain I misunderstood you," Anthony exclaimed. "Did you say *pregnant*?" The veterinarian slowly nodded, and Anthony continued on, evidently befuddled as he paced the floor. "She can't be. Surely you must be mistaken. The volunteer at the shelter assured us that Sugar had been spayed, and Spice was neutered a few weeks ago."

"Well, I'm sorry to break the news, but that volunteer was either sadly misinformed or urgently trying to seal the deal. If Spice and Sugar had any alone time together before he was neutered, he is most likely the father. Sugar is definitely not spayed. Either way, I'm almost positive this dog is having puppies. I'll take a blood sample to be sure, if you wouldn't mind waiting."

Chelsea and Anthony glimpsed at each other and then down at their dog, dumbfounded regarding their unforeseen predicament.

Chelsea spoke this time, a little more composed than her husband. "Yes, please, take a blood test. We don't have room for puppies. As you can probably tell by our reactions, we weren't expecting this."

The vet did as they asked and returned with the results a short while later. "I'm sorry to break the news, but it's just as I'd thought: Sugar is expecting."

"She's really pregnant?" Chelsea exclaimed in disbelief. "This is awful! What are our choices?"

"Well, as far as your options go, depending on how far along she is, you can have the pregnancy terminated. Or you can let her go full term and give the pups away or even sell them. Assuming that Spice is the father, people will pay top dollar for purebred duck tollers."

"What did you mean about terminating the pregnancy? Do you mean abort the pups? Is that really an option?"

The veterinarian nodded. "It is."

Chelsea and her husband exchanged glances, and after a moment of thought, they both shook their heads.

"We can't do that," Anthony said. After considering their predicament, he continued. "I guess we have no choice. We'll let her go full term and then sell the pups, providing they are purebreds. I can take out an ad in the classifieds. That sound okay with you, Chelsea?"

With slight hesitation, she agreed.

The veterinarian gave them a moment to gather their thoughts. "Okay, let me give her a full exam, and I'll get you the supplements that she'll require. It'll all work out. I have complete confidence that you'll both do fine."

Dr. Hill advised them that Sugar was about five weeks along in her pregnancy. She'd most likely give birth in another four weeks.

Once they arrived home, they talked it through, ironing out all of the nitty-gritty details. Since they were financially well off, they agreed that they would sell each pup and donate the proceeds to an animal rescue group.

On the advice of Dr. Hill, they set out to buy a few books on what to expect with an expecting dog. They had fallen in love with Sugar from the moment they set eyes on her, and they wanted to ensure that she was healthy, comfortable, and provided with everything she needed.

This would be the first time both Anthony and Chelsea would experience not only owning a pregnant dog, but also witnessing a delivery. They planned to be there for Sugar every step of the way. It was essential that they were carefully prepared.

In the midst of their conversations, they agreed on many different things, including one small yet very significant detail. No matter what the circumstances, no matter how irresistible the puppies were, neither of them would grow attached, and each one would be sold.

Chapter 3: Four Weeks Later

Whoever declared that love at first sight doesn't exist has never witnessed the purity of a puppy or looked deep into a puppy's eyes. If they did, their lives would change considerably.

First thing Monday morning, Sugar awoke and began panting and pacing more than normal. The pitter-patter of her frantic paws tapping against the ceramic tile woke everyone.

Chelsea and Anthony were prepared for this day and had set up a birthing area for her. When they realized that it was time, they directed her to it, distracting the expectant mom so that she wouldn't attempt to deliver her pups outside.

When she was almost ready, Sugar dug around in the blankets so that they were bunched into a comfortable pile. She then made an attempt to lie down and get into position.

Though it felt like forever and a day, Chelsea and Anthony remained by her side until the first tiny pup made her grand entrance into this big world. Due to her gentle disposition, Sugar exhibited no complaints when Chelsea tried to soothe her by scratching her gently behind the ears and whispering softly to her. Anthony massaged Sugar's back every so often, and she didn't mind one bit. In fact, they interpreted her reaction as pure appreciation judging by the way she moaned and nestled closer to her owner's hand.

As each precious pup was born, Sugar licked it lovingly to ensure the puppy was breathing before chewing the umbilical cord and preparing for the next birth.

Most of the pups were born within a half hour of each other, while the last two were born with an hour delay in-between. The young mother handled it like a trooper.

Toward the end, Sugar was clearly exhausted, but still maintained her natural ability to feed as necessary, licking each pup as they suckled and maintaining her gentle disposition by welcoming her owners' touch.

It was one in the afternoon by the time the last pup was born, a runt that was noticeably smaller than the rest.

All of the pups were born with mostly tan fur, fox-like ears, and a tiny white tuft centered in the front of their chest. All except for the runt, however, had tiny white patches on the tips of their webbed paws. They were a perfect combination of Sugar and Spice. Undoubtedly, Spice was the father.

Chelsea had asked Dr. Hill to make a special visit to their home afterward to make sure that Sugar and her pups were healthy and had all the medical care they required. Fortunately for them, it was a clean birth, free of any complications.

Just as Sugar was clearly spent, both Chelsea and Anthony were thoroughly fatigued. The stress and excitement from watching Sugar endure the delivery of six pups was enough to force them to retire early that evening.

Sugar remained with the pups, and Spice cuddled against the birthing pen like a gentle and proud father.

Chapter 4: Love at First Sight

Love is not something you can plan; it just happens naturally without warning.

During the eight weeks that followed, Chelsea and Anthony followed through with the pups' visits to the vet and were mostly pleased with the results. All of them were given a clean bill of health—except for the runt.

On her visit to the vet, the smallest was initially diagnosed with a bout of kennel cough, which Dr. Hill treated with antibiotics and carefully monitoring of her progress. It was a divine miracle that her littermates weren't afflicted with it, but the doctor explained that occasionally only one gets sick, while the others are not affected in the least.

The Sheltons considered themselves lucky.

Shortly after the pup had recovered from her first illness, her health took another turn for the worse. She contracted ringworm from an infected dog at the vet's office. Once again, she was given both oral and topical medications to send her on the road to recovery.

Finally, just when they thought the pup would never be well, Anthony and Chelsea received the news they had been dying to hear: she was free of any medical issues.

She was the last of the pups to be sold, as her siblings had buyers waiting for them when they were eight weeks old. Due to all of her illnesses, however, the couple wanted to wait a few months to sell her. It was more at Chelsea's insistence that they keep her for such a long time; she felt more comfortable waiting it out than risking selling a sick puppy. There was no reason to compromise her health unnecessarily.

During those months Chelsea started to feel the transition. She was breaking the cardinal rule that she and Anthony had discussed and had become attached to the pup.

She observed how gentle the runt was and how lovable she became. While most puppies are mischievous and constantly getting themselves into oodles of trouble, this pup was calm, obedient, and intelligent. It seemed that she picked up commands overnight. She didn't chew on furniture, slippers, or the walls, and was almost fully housebroken by five months. Most of her playtime was spent chasing after tennis balls or shaking her favorite stuffed duck back and forth. Her only downfall, if you could call it that, was demanding too much snuggle time by climbing into Chelsea's lap and curling up in a ball for a nap.

The three dogs—Sugar, Spice, and the runt—were inseparable. They ate together, played together, and, without fail, slept together.

Much to her chagrin, Chelsea felt herself falling hard for the runt. Since she was working only part time, she'd spend many of her days at home, alone with Sugar, Spice, and what they called "the little one."

In the beginning, they had refrained from giving her a name, but as Chelsea grew more attached, she secretly thought of one that was right for the pup, who resembled a fox when she ran in dizzying circles. So, when Anthony wasn't home, Chelsea referred to the pup as Foxy.

She didn't dare tell him, as they'd made a pact to remain unattached. A pact she felt herself break in half.

Foxy was going on six months old and, as is to be expected, she grew attached to Chelsea as well.

Though Chelsea and Anthony hated to see their pups depart, there was no feasible way that they could keep all of them. They already had their hands full with Sugar and

Spice, who shared a zest for life and a healthy dose of tireless energy. Adding a third one to the mix would only upset the apple cart and add havoc to their already busy lives.

Before Sugar delivered, Chelsea and Anthony tried to gauge what to expect. They scouted out other breeders to ask for their advice, who convinced them that it would be a piece of cake when the time came to sell. They declared that taking care of a litter of puppies is a full-time job, so when the right buyer came along, it would be a blessing in disguise.

"Think of all the money!" so many of them had said, like it was a quote derived straight out of the dog breeders' bible. Unfortunately, when the time came, Chelsea and her husband didn't share their enthusiasm.

When the couple had elected to allow Sugar to go full term, they didn't realize how difficult it would be to let the pups leave and venture off to new homes. Saying good-bye to each pup tore ferociously at their heartstrings.

In fact, immediately after the pups were weaned, Sugar was taken to the vet to be spayed. There were too many homeless dogs on the streets or in shelters, and Chelsea and Anthony didn't want to share any responsibility for adding more to the already dense population.

The months passed, and that dreadful day finally came. Foxy was going to be sold. Anthony had spoken to and screened the buyers over the phone, and he advised Chelsea that they seemed perfectly capable of taking care of the pup. She didn't have the heart to tell him how much she didn't want to sell her, but figured it would be for the best in the long run.

On this particular warm, summer day, Chelsea cradled the darling pup, knowing that today would be the last day she'd ever lay eyes on her warm, furry body.

The couple that Anthony had spoken with had finally arrived. Chelsea watched with tears in her eyes, nervously clasping her hands as if she were giving up her firstborn, as Glenn and Marybeth Kennedy walked up the driveway to meet the pup.

In many ways, she truly felt like she was giving up her daughter.

Anthony had sensed that Chelsea had grown attached, but she obdurately denied it. When they had first discovered Sugar's pregnancy, Chelsea had sworn that she would develop a tough skin. Clearly, she couldn't admit that she'd fallen in love...and that she'd actually named her.

"They seem like normal people," she exclaimed to her husband as he came up behind her and gave her a hug.

"I'm sure they're fine," he reassured her. "You worry too much. We discussed this, honey. We can't keep her." He nestled his face in her hair and whispered again in her ear. "She'll be in good hands."

"I know. I only want to make sure she gets a good home. I'm just being silly, I suppose."

She looked toward the pen containing the lone sleeping pup and nodded. "Okay, I'm ready. I guess we *should* let them in." She snickered at her own foolishness as she tried to regain her composure and prevent herself from crying. She should have known that this wouldn't be easy.

"Yeah, that's probably a good idea." Anthony was concerned that she would not let go. Though she may have outwardly denied her attachment, he knew her better than anyone. She had fallen hard.

Glenn and Marybeth weren't the first to express interest, and he knew that if Chelsea had her way, they'd never sell this one. In fact, if he didn't know any better, he'd think his wife had purposely gone out of her way to get the pup sick, just so she *could* keep her. But he knew she would never take it that far.

He had to be stern or Chelsea would reject these people, as she did the ones before...and the ones before them.

As the couple walked in, it was obvious that Marybeth was pregnant. She was a tall woman with dark brown hair puffed up like she had just walked off a movie set from the eighties. Her nails were neatly painted with shiny, bright red polish, and she wore black leggings that clung tightly to her legs with a red peasant shirt drooping over them. The bump for a belly showed that she had to be at least five months pregnant, but the rest of her was fit as a fiddle.

"Good morning! Glad you could make it!" Anthony greeted the couple and extended his hand. Chelsea followed his lead, but she eyed them up and down, trying to uncover their faults.

"Oh, we've been looking forward to it," Glenn said. "Especially Marybeth. When she read your ad in the paper, she perfected her nagging campaign." They all shared a chuckle as Anthony invited the couple into the house.

Glenn seemed like a friendly man. He had a full head of dark hair along with a thick, black, neatly groomed beard. He wasn't as flashy as his wife and dressed more like a construction worker, with jeans, a flannel shirt and work boots.

Chelsea tried to break the ice, though deep down she was resentful, knowing full well she had no reason to be. She pointed to the pup in the pen. "She really is growing every day. She was given a clean bill of health from the vet, and she has the hearty appetite to prove it."

"I can imagine. That makes two of us!" Marybeth rubbed her swollen belly.

Chelsea did her best to smile. "How far along are you?"

"Five months. Only four long months to go."

"Oh, it'll go by quickly, so I've heard." She thought about the baby that she'd never have and felt a brief wave of self-pity. She quickly dismissed it, believing that everything must happen for a reason. "I must say that you *are* courageous bringing a puppy into your household with a newborn on the way." As the words escaped her mouth, she prayed they weren't using this dog to test their parenting skills, and then cursed herself for thinking such a thing.

Marybeth didn't help matters. "Yeah, we're hoping to get some training in—for both us and the puppy—before our baby gets here. Hopefully, it'll give us a little insight into what we should expect. We look forward to her and our baby becoming the best of friends."

Anthony squeezed his wife's elbow, as he knew exactly what she was thinking. He was certain that she'd try to dissuade the couple from buying the pup if she thought for one minute they were buying it for a trial run. Anthony realized, perhaps more than Chelsea, that when selling puppies, they couldn't screen every buyer or read them the riot act. They had to trust that this couple would take good care of her. They were paying good money for her, after all.

For fear of scaring the couple, he only lightly touched upon their experience rather than ask twenty questions. "Have you owned a dog before?"

"Oh, yes, Marybeth's family has had a ton of dogs, and we had one or two while I was growing up."

"Perfect. Know much about the breed?"

"Sure, retriever, right?"

"Well, yeah, but she is called a Nova Scotia duck tolling retriever. A little different from a golden retriever."

"Really? Looks just like a golden," Marybeth chimed in as she bent down to get to the pup's level. She scratched Foxy under the chin and laughed it off when the pup ran off and cowered in the corner.

Disturbed by the pup's unusually timid behavior, Chelsea cut in and gave them the rundown while Anthony picked up the runt, who clung to his collar. "Duck tollers are the smallest of the retrievers and have a similar temperament. If raised properly, they do tend to be great with children."

As she spoke, Anthony continued to watch her carefully to make sure she didn't say anything inappropriate.

She continued. "They can be quite neurotic though, so it's important that they get plenty of exercise. They can't be cooped up, or they'll be miserable...and drag you down with them. Sitting stagnant is the worst thing for them. I assume you'll be able to exercise her a bit?"

"Oh, no problem there! I walk four miles a day. Once the baby arrives, I plan to get back into jogging. I'd love to have a companion for that." Marybeth patted her belly as she spoke, and her intentions seemed genuine.

Chelsea was a little relieved and softened up a bit.

Glenn turned toward his wife. "So, whatta ya think, babe? Shall we take this little girl to her new home?"

As Anthony passed the puppy to Marybeth to hold in her arms for the first time, Glenn knew he had his answer, even though the puppy squirmed in protest. "How much did you say she was?"

Anthony answered, assuming that Chelsea wouldn't. "Normally, this breed is sold for 1,700 dollars. Since she is a little older, we brought the price down to 1,500. Keep in mind, she's up to date with her shots and even microchipped. Though we didn't do that for all of our pups, given her age and the fact that she is quite a speedball of a runner, we decided better safe than sorry."

Glenn nodded and didn't haggle over the price. Once they completed the paperwork, they paid, nestled the pup in her own blankets, and left the house. Foxy whined uncontrollably as they exited the house.

Tears poured from Chelsea's eyes and streamed down her face as she watched them leave with Foxy.

"They'll be fine, honey. Let's not forget, we still have Sugar and Spice. They still need us." He gently kissed the top of her head and gave her a minute to herself.

She ignored Anthony and watched as the couple drove away out of sight. She felt as though someone had punched her in the chest and kicked her in the knees. She knew her heart would eventually mend, but she hadn't realize just how attached she'd grown to the little girl until that very moment.

In a whispered breath that held back sobs, she waved and cried, "Good-bye, Foxy." She silently prayed that the pup would be safe and loved in her new home, and she did her best to be happy for her. She hoped with all her heart that they'd sold her to the right couple.

Chapter 5: String of Lies

For every individual that practices lies and deceit, punishment patiently awaits them.

Once Glenn and Marybeth arrived home, Marybeth put the puppy down in the pen, kicked off her shoes, and smiled cunningly at her husband. "Think they bought it?" She then promptly removed the baby-sized pillow that was stuffed under her shirt. "I couldn't wait to take this thing off. I was so uncomfortable and hot. I don't know how anyone could carry a real baby for nine months. I was getting feverish in that house."

Ignoring his wife's overly dramatic complaints, he gently pulled at her arm. "Come here and kiss me. *You* were fantastic. You played that mommy role so flawlessly, *I* almost believed that you were pregnant. And I love the part about not really knowing which breed the dog was. Simply priceless."

As she inched closer to her husband, she was beaming. "I'm so excited about the money we're going to make once she produces some puppies. Remind me of how long we have to wait until we start breeding?"

"Logistically, we *should* wait until she's at least two years old, but like we do with all of our dogs, we start earlier. She's six months now. As soon as she goes into heat, she'll be ready. We still have all the others to keep us afloat for a few months. By that time, the golden will be ready, and then this prize duck toller will be next."

None of their dogs had names. They were all referred to by a serial number and the type of breed. The couple owned over fifty dogs, all different pedigrees, including a German shepherd and the golden retriever cramped in tiny crates that sat in a large, fenced area in the backyard. The new addition would be joining them shortly, as would newer dogs as they continued to build their empire.

"So, duck tollers generally produce six to ten pups? If we breed her two times per year, we'll be sitting on a pretty profit."

"Yep, that's what I'm talking about. Put her in the pen. Let's go celebrate. I didn't think that woman was ever going to let her go. Sheesh. Talk about attachment. I'm thankful her husband was there to make her relinquish control of the sale. Obviously he's the logical one."

"Oh, tell me about it. I could've sworn she knew I was faking the pregnancy. Eyed me up and down like a damn hawk. Thought she'd ask me for a blood test before we left. I couldn't wait to get out of there."

"Well, give yourself a pat on the back. We did it. Now we let Ernie know we need the stud, and we're all set."

Chapter 6: One Month Later

Evil and selfishness are the traits of many, which karma has bookmarked and which will inevitably tip the scales.

During the course of the past month, Glenn and Marybeth had made thousands off their various dogs. Forcing them to breed two times each in one year produced litters of between eight and ten pups for the larger dogs and between two and four for the smaller ones.

Buyers were easy to come by, as Glenn and Marybeth also owned the only pet shop in town—another of Glenn's well-thought-out investment.

Glenn was an experienced breeder, if you could call him that, and Marybeth was still learning the tricks of the trade. She quickly fell in love with the income it provided, not caring about the lives that had suffered for her selfish gain. Glenn aggrandized her intelligence and called her a fast learner, even though in truth, there wasn't much to learn. Glenn did most of the work.

They had just disposed of their aging Labrador bitch by dropping her off outside the nearest shelter after hours. They surmised that someone would pick her up and claimed that they were compassionate, as other puppy-mill owners simply killed their dogs when they were done with them. No, Glenn and Marybeth boasted that they were caring folk for giving their senior producers a chance to be adopted.

In reality, it's inconceivable to imagine how they could label themselves as caring, considering the poor conditions in which their dogs lived. All of the bitches were kept outside, hidden deep in the backyard, confined in a tiny pen that gave them only enough room to get up, turn around, do their business, and lie back down.

There were more than fifty cages, some stacked on top of others, providing less than adequate living conditions for the dogs.

Most of the dogs were covered with dirt, urine, and feces. And they were left to battle the harsh elements, regardless if the weather was glacially frigid or blistering hot.

Exercise was rare and only granted when the owners cleaned up the pen. Sometimes a week passed before they were cleaned, and even then it was only to prevent complaints from the neighbors.

Long before the dogs ended up at the mill, they all had beautiful fur, which was now nothing more than a collection of filthy, matted knots; since their capture, baths and brushing were out of the question. Some of them were balding due to the substandard circumstances.

They were fed the cheapest of food, sometimes subsisting off mere scrapings off the ground, depriving them of the proper nutrients necessary for growth and good health.

Should any of the bitches become sick, they'd only be tended to if the veterinarian's cost was minimal and they were worth it—meaning they produced decent-sized litters. Any costs that exceeded the couple's cheap budget would result in euthanasia for the dog, which would be hastily replaced with another bitch of the same breed. If the dog was lucky, the euthanasia was humane.

The only time the expectant mother was given special attention was when she was about to deliver and when the puppies were born. Glenn allowed her to nurse her pups and kept them warm in an old, small trailer on the premises for that purpose. The moment the puppies were old enough to be legally sold at the pet store, they were ripped away from their mother and displayed in the front window of the shop so unsuspecting passersby couldn't resist.

Marybeth always smiled when she watched the buyers shell out their hard-earned cash to buy the irresistible puppies. Most customers were clueless that the puppies were born in such a horrifying environment and that their mothers were living a life of hell.

If you could call it living.

It wasn't an accident that the pet store was directly across the street from a toy shop. This was by design, giving Marybeth and Glenn—the pet store owners—the distinct advantage to observe young children tug on their parents' coat sleeves as they begged for a darling little puppy and then watch their parent oblige.

Nine times out of ten, the child got what he or she wanted, and another puppy was sold at top dollar. After all, who could resist the persistence of a wailing, young child?

Genuine opportunists, Glenn and Marybeth had been making a living off the sale of pup, and were planning to retire at an early age, though their house was far from paid off. With all the money that they made, it was surprising that they weren't savvy enough to adhere to a proper budget. Yet they were penny conscious in some ways. For example, they hadn't found it necessary to buy a bitch in quite a few years, because they were able to get most breeds from an animal shelter.

It was astounding how many purebred puppies were just thrown away like yesterday's garbage. Glenn and Marybeth were more than happy to pick those "freebies" up and put them to good use in ways that benefited them.

They had to make concessions in Foxy's case, as duck tollers were difficult to come by. Some customers had been requesting duck toller puppies, and like the money-hungry store owners that they were, they made good on their promise to deliver. It was no sweat off their back, really, as they'd double their profits in no time, making their return on investment worth every penny…and then some.

Once the duck toller was ready to breed, they notified their contact, who owned a handsome stud, and geared up to put the plan in motion.

Foxy's pen was no different from the others, except for a few bricks lining the bottom portion. As the original owners had cautioned, she was a runner and did so at any given chance. They didn't want to give her an opportunity to dig her way to freedom. As a matter of fact, the wire crate was helpful to them, as it often stripped the fur off the ankles of poor dog, making it too painful to run far.

Glenn and Marybeth never considered the overall well-being of their dogs; they only cared that they produced. In their minds, a few cuts and bruises were nothing to concern themselves with. If it didn't affect them directly, they paid no mind to it. This was the motto by which they lived their lives, with dogs and humans alike.

Chapter 7: Profits

A dog's broken heart can be mended only by those who know the true beauty inside.

When Foxy turned seven months old and was in season, Glenn called his trusted acquaintance, Ernie, to deliver the stud and pair the dogs. After becoming acquainted, the female and the stud were left alone for some quality time and privacy.

As could be expected, Glenn acted like a peeping Tom whenever he could, a slideshow of scrolling dollar signs sparkling in his Machiavellian eyes. Marybeth manned the shop, eagerly waiting for that phone call in anticipation of good news.

The stud stayed for a little over a week before returning home to his owner, and it appeared the two got along shamelessly.

After three weeks, Glenn extracted a blood sample from the bitch and used his canine pregnancy test to reveal the results. As he'd hoped, the dog was indeed pregnant.

He called his wife at the shop. "Marybeth, guess what, darlin'? We're expecting!" Ernie was second on the speed dial and was thrilled to hear about it, boasting loudly about his dog's natural ability to breed. A litter of puppies meant profit for him. His work was done; now all he had to do was sit back, relax, and collect the reward.

Glenn marched Foxy back to her lonely crate and slammed the door behind her. "Good job, dog. You'd better produce a decent litter with some good-looking puppies."

She watched her owner leave and paced the wire crate until the bottom of her paws began to bleed. She yelped in pain, but, as usual, no one was there to help her. Without any other option, she curled up in a ball and licked her wounds, longing for the love of her first owner, who used to cradle her in her arms and gently kiss the top of her fluffy head.

As she closed her eyes, she tried to remember the scent of that kind woman and the feel of her soft hands as she stroked her back, underneath her chin, and behind her tiny, pointed ears.

If she listened closely enough, she could hear the soothing hum that the woman used to sing before tucking her in her crate at night. That particular crate was a good memory of a cushioned bed, with a variety of stuffed animals and her biological parents sleeping right outside of it.

The memory coaxed her into sleep, even with the continuous barking of the other lonely dogs and the cold rain that fell on her, saturating her now bedraggled coat.

She hoped that somehow she would awaken back at the one special place she knew as her home.

Chapter 8: Divine Loyalty

A dog instinctively exercises loyalty; if only people would do the same.

Within nine weeks, Foxy exhibited signs that she was ready to give birth. With as much tenderness as someone taking out the garbage, Glenn led her over to the old trailer, where ratty blankets were left for her to deliver her pups on.

As he did with all his expectant mothers, he left her alone, still just a puppy herself, to tend to the newborn pups without anyone to soothe her during the birthing process. Every now and again, Glenn popped his head in to make sure all the puppies survived and grinned proudly as he watched his new prize nurse six of the seven puppies.

She watched closely as Glenn entered the trailer, and her eyes followed him as he left. Initially, she blindly hoped he'd come over to assure her, pet her, or maybe just scratch her behind the ears or give her a belly rub to soothe her swelling, but he did none of that.

She aimed to please him, as it was in her nature to be a loyal dog and obey her master, but as more time lapsed and as her puppies grew bigger, she only looked forward to seeing him because it meant being fed, even though it wasn't much of a feeding. Other than that, she didn't long to see him at all.

Day by day, Glenn came in, and each day her puppies grew just a little bigger, all except for one. The firstborn had a less hearty appetite than the others and wasn't quite as alert. He often slept in the corner, rarely getting up to play with his littermates. When he did eat, it was barely enough to quench his thirst.

Foxy watched solemnly as Glenn took her puppies away individually as they grew older, and she whimpered softly as the last one was removed, as this one was indeed her firstborn.

But Glenn didn't handle this last one gently. This pup hadn't made it after all, regardless of all his mom's attempts to revive him. Foxy licked the still pup's small mouth and face in an attempt to breathe life into him, but Glenn's cold hand grabbed him from her reach, not showing so much as an ounce of remorse. He threw the small pup in a tiny plastic bag.

Sadly, only six of the litter had survived, and Foxy mourned by herself in silence as she started to understand the cruelty of the world as she now knew it.

Chapter 9: Six Months Later

Why doesn't somebody do something? Thankfully there are those who can be the "somebody" that everyone else always refers to.

Six months had passed since Foxy delivered her first litter and Glenn reckoned she was ready to mate again. It was Sunday afternoon, and Glenn was excited to get the ball rolling. Ernie and his stud had recently moved out of state, but like the resourceful entrepreneur that Glenn was, he had another duck toller stud all lined up to pair with his bitch.

He called his pal, Jerry, first thing and told him that he should come by and drop off the stud. He was sure the two dogs would take an immediate liking to each other, since he had such good luck the first time. He had no reason to believe that his female would be anything but gentle, docile, and agreeable. He was confident she'd behave affably.

The male, named Bentley was a bit of a handful, friskier than the female. Since he was still young, his main objective in life was simply to play. Since Jerry had never used Bentley for breeding, the dog had lived a very normal life, getting the nutrients, medication, exercise, and love he required. The environment in which he was raised was a healthy one, where he was properly socialized and loved, unlike that of the meek female.

When Jerry and Bentley arrived, Jerry looked around the peculiar surroundings. He'd never bred a dog before, and it was not quite what he'd expected, nor did it fit Glenn's lavish description. Glenn had assured him that he was a licensed breeder. At first glance, it was evident that the yard was too rundown to belong to a breeder.

The entire backyard was nothing but a collection of dirt and rocks, complete with one tree that drooped over the rows of crates. While the front of the house was impeccable, it was a classic case of false advertising.

There was no question. This had to be either a backyard breeder or a puppy mill.

Now vigilant and unsure of how to proceed, Jerry took Bentley into the yard and allowed his mind to sort things out while the dogs were introduced. He knew that he could always leave at his discretion, and he wanted to be absolutely certain that he wasn't jumping to conclusions. After all, he tended to do that from time to time, but his instincts broadcasted warning signals loud and clear.

He had known Glenn only for a short time, and truthfully, he wasn't overly crazy about him. But he'd thought breeding his dog would be an exciting and unforgettable experience. Suddenly, he was having second thoughts.

When the dogs were first introduced, the female cowered in the corner, not sure of what to expect from the bubbly whirlwind of energy otherwise referred to as Bentley. He, on the other hand, did what was considered mannerly in dog world and gravitated toward her hindquarters, for which he was immediately greeted with a warning growl, followed by a feisty snap.

While the female was terrified, Bentley was having the time of his life circling the small pen and invading the female's personal space.

Jerry was confident the two would become fast friends in good time, but Glenn's frustration was obvious. It was so obvious that Jerry became agitated and immediately regretted his decision. He didn't have to put any more thought into it. Glenn's explanation of his business was nothing more than an embellished fabrication that was light-years away from the truth.

"They'll be fine, Glenn," Jerry said with marked annoyance. "They just need some quality time to get acquainted."

"Time is money, Jerry. Don't you know anything?" Glenn snapped at his friend. Leaving the two dogs in the pen, Glenn stormed off into the house to get Marybeth, and both came back out, their annoyance displayed by scowls that enhanced the voluminous frown lines deeply etched in their faces.

Feeling more than uncomfortable with his friend's unwarranted temper, the lies, and the entire situation in a nutshell, Jerry removed his venturesome dog from the pen, buying time and claiming that perhaps they'd get along better if Bentley was exercised and calm. He promised he'd bring Bentley back after the dog's morning walk.

It was a promise he had no intention of keeping.

The truth was that once Jerry had done a thorough reconnaissance of the entire yard, he felt sickened. Once he allowed it to sink in and realized what it was, his heart broke when he thought of all the torment those innocent dogs had endured and would continue to endure if no one stepped in to help.

Though he didn't get close enough to all of them, he had read enough about puppy mills to envisage what they looked like. The female duck toller looked as though she hadn't had a bath in years, and it also looked like her legs had fur missing. Abrasions covered portions of her thin body.

Circumspectly, Jerry weighed his options and watched as his supposed friend displayed genuine anger, kicking up dirt and behaving like a spoiled five-year-old that had dropped his lollipop for the sixth time.

Anger bubbled through his own veins, and his heart crumbled at the thought of that precious dog cooped up without a morsel of love. He wanted to call Glenn out on his lies, but he thought it best to leave.

Jerry and Bentley made their way his truck. The yard gate banged shut behind them and then bounced back open. As Jerry glanced back, he noticed the lock hadn't latch as it should have. His first impulse was to pull the gate closed, but his mind quickly shifted, and he realized exactly what he had to do. The devil and an angel on his shoulders were having a disagreement, and this time the devil won.

Or the angel, depending on how you look at it.

Every dog deserves the opportunity to be in a loving environment, Jerry thought, *and none should have to live like those poor dogs in such cramped quarters*. That alone prompted him to leave the gate open about six inches—just enough room for a dog to escape should she feel the need. Any of those dogs would be safer roaming the streets than under the care of Glenn and Marybeth Kennedy.

Jerry didn't want to remain in the same circle as someone with such little compassion or regard for an animal's life. As he opened the truck door for Bentley, he said, "Come on, Bentley. Let's get the heck out of here. I'm sorry I even put you through this. You're getting a *huge* rawhide when you get home!"

The angelic dog wagged his tail at the sound of his name, not realizing how lucky he was.

Jerry didn't know what his next steps would be, but he knew with every fiber of his being that he had to take action one way or the other. He now was on an urgent mission to help those poor dogs and be the boisterous voice for all of those without one.

He did know that one of the first things he would do would be to get Bentley neutered. He'd then proceed from there.

Chapter 10: Freedom Found

A dog's heart should dance in a waltz of happiness, not flutter in a tango of fear.

Lori Jamison and her mother were returning from an ordinary trip to the grocery store, making idle chitchat the way an awkward teenager and her mother normally do. Typically, they had a good relationship, but recently they seemed to be drifting apart.

They'd been thrashing through some turbulent waters lately, especially since the youngest member of the family turned three years old.

Nathan was a loving little boy, but he had abruptly developed a rare respiratory disorder. The doctors had been working with the family since the beginning of the year and were still running tests to try to diagnose his symptoms.

The continuous uncertainty and mind-boggling fear of the unknown caused a strain on Patricia and her husband, as well as their two daughters, Lori and Melissa. The four of them were consistently uptight, concerned about Nathan's health and having to shift plans whenever Nathan had an episode that compromised his breathing.

Lori was the oldest and was acting like quite the rebel. The previous week, she had been caught with a small bag of marijuana, a drug her parents used to dabble in themselves, but in no way condoned for their own children. She was generally a good kid, and Patricia was confident that she could nip it in the bud before it became a deeper issue. But it was never the right time to have that serious conversation with her daughter.

When she finally established the nerve to speak to Lori during their drive home, it was going exceptionally well until Lori interrupted and squealed, "Mom, stop!"

"What? Oh my goodness!" She saw a small ball of fur jolt in front of her car and slammed on her brakes just in time. Her front tire stopped no more than one foot away from the fleeing dog.

Both mother and daughter flung open the SUV's doors and jumped out of the truck to make sure the dog was unharmed. Thankfully, she didn't appear injured, but she was frightened and quivered as she crawled away from Patricia and underneath the truck

Her light-brown eyes shifted back and forth between Lori and Patricia; she was scared to move so much as an inch.

Patricia knelt down, as Lori kept lookout, making sure that no other drivers passed by. Fortunately, the incident had occurred on a quiet street. If the startled dog were to take flight into a major intersection, it would all be over.

"Come on, girl." Patricia slowly held her hand out and spoke softly, trying to lure the dog to safety, but the dog wouldn't budge. Quietly, Patricia got Lori's attention. "Go into the back and get some crackers out of the grocery bags." For the first time in a while, Lori did exactly as she was told without putting up a fight.

"Here." She was used to shouting at her mom for every little thing, but managed to soften her tone as she handed her mom the crackers, realizing that any strident noise could send the startled dog off in a frenzy.

Patricia held out her hand to the dog and seemed to have won her attention, at least for the moment. The dog was obviously hungry, but its fear was far greater than its desire to eat. It looked behind her, then at the big tires that almost ended her life, and then in front of her, her expressive eyes transfixed on the delicious snack nestled in the strange woman's hands.

If it were possible for any dog to calculate the time it took to run and grab a cracker and then retreat back to safety, this dog was a seasoned mathematician. She wondered if this woman would be anything like her original owner—nurturing and kind. Though she was scared, the woman's voice was soft and almost reassuring, something the dog hadn't experienced in a very long time.

She decided to give it a try and took one step toward Patricia. Then she slowly and cautiously took another. Patricia held her hand up, motioning for Lori to stay away until she could entice the dog out and get a firm hold on her. She couldn't tell if the dog was wearing a collar, its fur was so matted.

The dog inched closer, each move thoroughly guarded. It seemed like hours before she finally got close enough to almost touch. Patricia inched backward just a bit. She wanted Lori to be able to sneak in if necessary and grab the dog.

Lori was focused and in full cooperation.

As the dog advanced one more step closer, Patricia reached out with an open palm for her to take the cracker, while Lori cleverly sneaked up behind her.

Between the two of them, they were able to grasp the writhing dog and lift it safely into the truck.

Lori flew into the backseat with the dog, while Patricia quickly shut the door behind them and climbed back into the driver's seat. While still traumatized, the dog lay down, but her gaunt body trembled. She looked around, her eyes wide and her tiny ears pinned back, carefully studying her new surroundings.

"You okay back there?" Patricia asked Lori while trying to catch her breath.

"Yeah, you?" Lori answered while trying to gain the trust of the fearful dog.

"A few scratches, nothing critical."

The mother and daughter took a moment and both caught their breath. "Now what, Mom?"

"Well, we try to find her owner. Is she wearing a collar?" Patricia started to drive away, not quite sure yet where she was going.

Lori hadn't even thought to look for a collar. At first the dog didn't appear to be wearing one, until Lori carefully ran her fingers along the dog's neck. "Oh my god, mom. She has no tags, but she's wearing a collar. It's digging into her skin, practically strangling her."

"Well, take it off!"

"I can't wedge my fingers underneath it to get at the buckle or the clasp. It's too tight."

"What? It's too tight? What do you mean?" Patricia turned around when they stopped at the stoplight to get a closer look. "Oh, Lord, I'm surprised she can even breathe. There's a vet down the street. Let's take her there, remove that awful collar, and at least see if she's got a microchip in her."

"What in the world is a microchip?" Lori asked as she gently smoothed her hands down the dog's back. The frightened dog looked up at her, validating her curiosity and fear but didn't try to move away from her touch.

Not all hope was lost. She was making progress already.

Patricia began driving toward the vet's office. "It's a computerized chip with and identification number that they insert under the dog's skin with a large needle. The number is registered with one of a few companies that handle microchips, which has information about the owner, including a phone number. To find out the number, vets use scanners. I suppose it's sort of new—only been around for the past ten or fifteen years."

"Neat. Although I am not sure what kind of owner would leave a collar on like this. She can hardly breathe."

"No kidding. Not a very good one. You've done good, kid."

"Ugh, whatever." Secretly, she was pleased with the praise, and she prayed they couldn't find the owner.

She hoped they could finally have a dog.

Chapter 11: Blessed Discoveries

Trust, once it's discovered, is a precious emotion felt with the heart. It is so delicate that it can be both found and lost forever within mere seconds.

When they arrived at the vet, the doctor introduced herself as Dr. Fredericks and was very kind. She listened to Patricia and Lori describe how the dog ran directly in front of their truck and examined the collar that was wrapped tightly around its neck.

Dr. Fredericks was a petite woman but had the confidence of a lion. She was intelligent, informative, and most of all compassionate, especially toward the dog.

She asked them both to wait in the small room while she led the dog into the back. The vet techs restrained it, while she immediately removed the metal collar with a set of sharp clippers. Once removed, there was an actual indentation where the collar slightly punctured the skin and it began to bleed a little. The vet carefully covered the wound with topical medicine and applied white gauze and a bandage before taking the dog back into the room.

The vet noticed that the dog's fur was completely matted. Her tiny toes were scarred, and dried blood was generously caked on the bottom portion of her ankle. She assumed it was most likely the result of being confined in a wired-floored cage, but didn't want to jump to any conclusions just yet.

"Well, thank God the two of you came along when you did. A few more pounds on this dog and that collar would have engraved itself thoroughly into her skin. I've seen this type of thing before. That's what happens when the owner never removes the collar yet the dog continues to grow—a sure sign of neglect if you ask me. The good news is she's got a chip in her. It's registered to an owner. Mr. and Mrs. Anthony Shelton."

Lori couldn't help but frown and roll her eyes behind her mother's back. She was hoping the vet would have told them something different. From the looks of the dog, the owner was clearly negligent.

"Well, that's a start!" Patricia exclaimed. "Is there a phone number?"

The veterinarian looked up the microchip's registry. "Sure, it's right here. I'll call the one listed. Wait here."

When the doctor came back out into the waiting room, she looked slightly aggravated. "Well, the chip was registered to the Sheltons, but they are no longer the owners. The gentleman that answered gave me the number to the new owners. I called them, and they gave me their address." She hesitated as if she didn't want to say any more. "They said just to open the gate and put her in the yard. The gate is unlocked."

The vet knew the dog was emaciated and clearly undernourished. A nervous temperament is often viewed as an indication that a dog has been abused, and the way she crouched down when stroked suggested that she was petrified of human contact.

"They're not going to greet us there? Weren't they worried in the least?" Lori was disgusted, as was her mother and the doctor.

"I thought the same thing, to be honest. But it's not my place to judge. From the looks of it, this dog needs some major medical attention. Its situations like these that pain me the most. There's not much I can do except call animal control and let them make the determination."

"Can we do that?"

"Well, sure, I suppose. I'd recommend returning her and then calling. Since the dog just ran away, the owners will probably claim that she only appears to be neglected because she's been on the run. Give it a week. Then call. This way the dog's been home, and the owners will have no excuse for her shabby appearance. If she still looks the same way, then animal control can step in. Here's a leash. You'll probably need it." The pleasant doctor slipped the small, pink medical leash over the dog's head and handed Patricia the handle as well as the owner's address.

"Thank you so much, Dr. Fredericks. We truly appreciate your help."

"Any time. I hope I'm wrong. My wish is that this dog is returned to a loving home. I've just seen too many of these instances that prove otherwise. Until the laws get stricter, our hands are tied legally."

Patricia and Lori nodded in understanding. The laws that protected animals had always been inadequate, resulting in a mere slap on the wrist for the offenders.

As they left, they thanked the doctor and made their way to the owner's home. When they pulled into the long driveway of the address the doctor had written down, Patricia wanted nothing more than to back out and go back the way they had come.

The large ranch in itself was enchanting, as was the front yard. Lilacs decorated the walkway as plush bushes accentuated the ground under the front windows. A decorative flag with vibrant flowers painted on it hung from the metal flag post on the wraparound porch. A double swing sat underneath the maple tree in the middle of the humongous front yard.

While at first glance the house was beautiful, the substandard backyard broke Patricia's heart in two. At first glance, it looked like any normal backyard. But in the distance, she could see rows of cages and heard whimpering dogs.

Within seconds, Patricia realized what this place was, but unfortunately, there was nothing she could do about it. In the back of the dirt-filled yard, she saw three sets of cages with what appeared to be German shepherds and golden retrievers and then a few empty cages, one of which likely was for the dog they'd rescued.

Beyond that, further than her vision would allow her to see clearly, were rows of cages, presumably housing other dogs.

"Mom, forget it. Let's say she ran away and take her home. Come on, look at this place. It's a backyard breeder or a damn puppy mill. Look at those cages. Those poor dogs!"

"I know what it is, Lori, but we can't just steal a dog," Patricia whispered.

"Why not?"

"Because I'm quite certain stealing is against the law. And keep your voice down. They'll hear you. If we steal one of their prized possessions, don't you think there will be ramifications? Do you think they're just going to let it go?"

"What the hell are they going to do to us? Who's going to know? No one's here." Lori waved her arms around. "What kind of person loses a dog and isn't home to greet it when she's returned? They don't care about her. Look at the yard—it's covered with nothing but dirt and rocks. They live in cages. It's despicable! Mom, come on."

"Lori, I don't like it either, but we have to do what's right."

"Yeah, for whom? Because I can tell you one thing. It's certainly not right for this dog, and it's not right for all of them!" She motioned with one arm violently toward the cages in the yard.

Her mom shot her a look. The rebellious Lori was back again. It just so happened that the rebellious Lori was also a die-hard animal lover.

"Open the gate for me, please."

"No."

"What?"

"No. I'm not taking any part in this. You want to return the dog to eternity in a living hell, be my guest." Lori walked back to the car and got into the backseat, not wanting to sit anywhere near her mother.

Patricia cringed as she did so, but moved forward with the shaking dog, opened the gate, and put the dog down. The dog pawed at it and yelped, trying to grasp Patricia while she tried to close the gate behind her. "I'm sorry, girl. This is where you live." She looked around for the owners, but Lori was right. They were nowhere to be found. A single tear fell from her eye as the gate clanged shut.

She could hear the dog's yelps as she walked back toward their car. She tried her best to ignore them, not even looking back to make sure that the gate had latched into a locked position.

When Patricia got in the car, Lori started in right away, rubbing it in as much as possible. "Happy now?"

"No, Lori, and I don't like your tone. We did the right thing."

"No, you did your version of the right thing. I'm telling you, it was the wrong thing."

"Enough!"

"Whatever."

Tears stung in Patricia's eyes. Though she knew she did what was legally correct, emotionally it was one of the worst things she could've done. She returned an innocent dog to the one place for which she probably never would want to return. It was the one place she most likely worked diligently to escape. She only hoped that the dog wouldn't face any harsh punishment for her escape. The thought made her shudder with regret.

Patricia and Lori sat in silence as they backed out of the driveway. They turned toward home and stopped for a traffic jam only yards from the puppy mill.

Lori looked out the rear window, wallowing in anger, while Patricia caught a glimpse in the rearview mirror. They both saw it at the same time. "Mom!"

"I see her!"

The determined dog had escaped again and frantically raced at maximum speed straight in their direction. Before Patricia had a chance to speak, Lori had the same bag of crackers and jumped out of the car in the middle of traffic in an attempt to lure the pup back in.

Instead of refusing assistance, the dog bypassed Lori, bypassed the bag of crackers, and flew into the backseat of the truck, her tiny heart fluttering like a frightened bird. Lori was right behind her. She hugged her tight as she got into the backseat with her. The dog didn't flinch, growl, or object in any way.

With as stern a voice as she could muster, she warned her own mother, "Don't you even think about it, Mom."

Looking forward, Patricia smirked and said to herself, *I wasn't. Not on your life.* She was just thrilled to have been given a second chance and thankful that the dog was persistent enough to escape for the last time.

She was determined to help this dog; there was no way she'd return her now.

Chapter 12: The Road to Recovery

Some of us are meant to fly...and are eternally grateful when granted the wings to take flight.

Lori and Patricia arrived at their house with a very diffident and frightened young dog accompanying them. Neither was sure what the next steps would be, especially when taking Nathan's respiratory issues into consideration. All they knew was that they didn't want to take the dog back to that horrid place.

Her teeth, the ones that still existed, were brown and covered in tartar, while others were cracked in half, resulting in breath that reeked of dead fish.

As they sat in the truck, still parked on the driveway, Patricia had second thoughts. "Lori, Nathan is never going to be able to breathe around this dog the way she is. She's in desperate need of a good grooming. For all we know, she could be full of ticks, fleas, and whatever else."

"You're right," Lori replied. "Let's go back to the veterinarian's office."

Patricia deliberated about that option for a moment.

Knowing her mother well enough to read her thoughts, Lori interjected. "Mom, I seriously don't think she's going to call the owners. She looked just as upset and disgusted as we were. If she so much as mentions calling them, we leave. But I think she'll be more than happy to give this baby what she needs. This poor dog looks like she's been through hell. Gosh, how old can she be?"

"I don't know. I'd say a year or two, but she looks more like she is going on six or seven."

She looked at the dog one more time, reached her hand over the backseat to pet her. The dog raised her head and licked the palm of Patricia's hand. "Okay, let's get back to Dr. Fredericks. I hope she still has some wiggle room in her schedule today."

Once they arrived, the veterinarian gave them an amused, inquisitive smirk, but didn't say a word or ask any questions about what had happened since they'd left. And neither Lori nor her mother offered any additional information. They were content to let the doctor come to her own conclusions.

Lori spoke first, not wanting to waste any more time, wanting to get the dog on the road to recovery quickly. "She needs a bath, and a checkup...and I think she needs her teeth cleaned."

The veterinarian gave the dog a quick once-over and filled out the paperwork with the price quote. "You're absolutely right. She will definitely need a dental, and certainly a bath. She has fleas, not surprisingly, and a few ticks from what I can tell. Not the worst that I've ever seen, but unquestionably not the best." The doctor reached across to feel the dog's ribs. "She's a bit emaciated and dehydrated. You can tell if you touch here." She led Lori's hand to the dog's ribcage. "It wouldn't hurt to give her a full checkup with blood work. That is, if you'd like me to. And, one more thing, she's not spayed. Would you like me to take care of that?"

Patricia made a decent salary and donated to animal rescue each year. She figured instead of donating this year, the money could go toward helping this dog. Even if they decided not to keep her, she wanted to help out however she could. It was the least she could do. She felt that the poor dog had probably produced too many litters already; this was a no-brainer. "Yes, please. I'd appreciate if you can take blood work and spay her."

"Okay, the price with the bath, including the flea and tick dip, the spaying, blood work, and dental will come to..." The vet punched all of the details into the computer to calculate a price. "It'll be roughly one thousand dollars." Admiring the generosity of her new clients and realizing it wasn't even their dog, she said, "Given the circumstances of this poor dog's health, I'd be more than happy to split the price with you, so five hundred and we'll call it even."

"Seriously?" Patricia exclaimed. "Thank you so much, Dr. Fredericks. That is so gracious of you! When can we expect to pick her up?"

"Well, it's almost three now. Let me keep her overnight. We have an overnight staff that handles emergencies and keeps an eye on the place. I'll do the surgery first thing in the morning. She should be ready by three tomorrow afternoon, a little groggy, but good as new."

During the course of the evening, Patricia had a chance to speak to her husband, Braden, about the dog. She explained the almost grave circumstance under which they found her and, even worse, the dreadful place where they almost returned her. As soon as Patricia described where the dog had been living, Braden agreed to give it a shot, with the stipulation that they take her to a shelter if Nathan couldn't handle it.

Both Patricia and Lori were elated. Melissa was excited at the concept, and Nathan was simply too young to understand, but they were sure he would be ecstatic to have a live-in playmate.

When they picked up the dog the following day, they hardly recognized her. It was as if she'd been given a full makeover. Her knotted fur had been shaved down so that all of the ticks and fleas were thoroughly removed and any scarring or infection was properly medicated with topical ointments and antibiotics.

Her teeth were now only slightly yellow instead of black and caked with tartar, though one or two had been removed. They were far better than expected.

Dr. Fredericks said that her skin was in terrible condition, which perplexed her, because fleas and ticks were uncommon in Las Vegas. That could only mean that the facility from which she had come was worse than she had originally anticipated.

She estimated the dog's age to be about one and a half or two years. She also confirmed that the dog was completely undernourished, but gave them a special diet, including nutrients to "fatten her up" and put her on the road to recovery. She also gave them detailed information on post-operative instructions.

While the dog was still a bit loopy, she wobbled to the truck, and Lori helped her in. She slept the entire way home, finally able to relax in the hands of a caring family.

Chapter 13: Sweet Revenge

At one point or another, everyone gets what they deserve...good or bad.

By the time Glenn had realized his prized possession had flown the coup and had not been returned as instructed, he was utterly outraged. He was accustomed to everyone following his orders precisely as they are given, and he didn't handle any deviation well.

In no way could he ever be held accountable for anything in life, so he called his wife at the shop and roared accusations at her when she answered, assuming she was the one responsible for leaving the gate open.

After he hung up on her, he called the local shelters and veterinarian's offices on a mission to find his dog, each claiming they hadn't seen her but would keep a conscious lookout. Even Dr. Fredericks, who smiled through the whole conversation, petting *his* dog, told him she hadn't seen a dog matching that description. Then she slammed down the receiver and cursed him out, utilizing almost every obscenity in existence.

Losing this type of dog was a major setback for a thrifty entrepreneur, as it meant a substantial loss of profit, and Glenn was certainly all about the money.

In his typical frenzied tantrum, he phoned Jerry, who claimed he knew nothing of the dog's whereabouts or how the gate was left open. Jerry performed his clumsy version of a happy dance at the fact that the dog had escaped. He only hoped she had fallen into good hands.

Glenn fired cheap, irrational shots at him, claiming it was his fault, since Bentley and his dog hadn't hit it off. "If your dog would've just calmed himself down, *my* dog would be pregnant right now instead of roaming the streets! What kind of dog owner are you anyway? Raising a stud to be mischievous? You know what'll fix that? A good swift kick, that's what!"

Jerry hung up to avoid hearing the remainder of Glenn's verbal lashing.

All that phone call did was cause Jerry to acknowledge that leaving the gate open wasn't enough. He knew he'd better get his plan in motion. There were more dogs that needed to be rescued from Glenn's wrath. He had a job to do and thought he might know exactly who could help him with it.

Feeling an overwhelming sense of loathing for his old pal, he picked up the receiver and made a few phone calls to his tight-knit, dog-loving group of friends. After hearing the news, they were more than willing to help and agreed to meet for breakfast to formulate a foolproof plan.

If anyone could pull it off, it would be them.

Chapter 14: Loving Introductions

If someone doesn't see the good in you, you may want to consider the source.

When Patricia and Lori arrived home with the newest family member, the rest of the family was waiting eagerly by the front door. The dog was still drugged from the surgeries, but she slowly wagged her tail as she staggered with Patricia to the front step.

Braden held Nathan in his arms, while Melissa bent down to greet the shy and drowsy but incredibly charming pup. While she pet her, she looked up at her mom, "So, what's her name?"

"Oh, yeah, a name. I was so busy getting her to look presentable, I forgot about that."

Braden asked, "Didn't you say there was a collar on her?"

"Yeah, some collar," Lori said. "It was digging into her skin. Can you imagine? The only engraving in the nametag were the words 'duck toller' and the number 7609. They never even gave this poor dog a name. For her entire stay at that hellhole, she was nameless."

Nathan wiggled out of his father's arms and warily approached the dog. Patricia placed her hand over the dog's mouth, just in case she had a fear of children, as some rescue dogs do, and especially because she'd just gone through surgery.

To her amazement, the dog reacted completely the opposite of how she'd expected. As Nathan reached out to her, she widened her tired eyes, relaxed her body even more, and gave a slight thump of her tail, which was all she could muster in her somnolent state. As the young boy stepped in closer, the dog became even happier. Nathan squealed with delight as she nestled closer to him and gave a single lick to his face before once again closing her eyes.

Nathan's entire face lit up.

Braden was in shock. "Wow, I guess *someone* found a new friend!" Both Braden and Patricia shared a warm glance. Nathan not only battled a mystifying pulmonary disease, but he was generally a very taciturn boy, and it worried them that he may never fully come out of his shell.

"Wow, this dog didn't even give me the time of day, compared to how she reacts with Nathan," Melissa said.

"Oh, Melissa, she'll get used to you," Lori said. "She's still exhausted from the surgery. Give her a chance."

Nathan clapped his hands and smiled, his blue eyes twinkling as the dog continued to cuddle closer to him. "Look, Mom, it's Dixie!" Dixie was a dog on a cartoon that he frequently watched.

"She does look like her, doesn't she, Nathan!"

"Dixie likes me, Mom!"

The other family members looked at each other and nodded. Patricia exclaimed, "Dixie it is!"

The entire family had fallen hopelessly in love with her. She was undeniably bashful, and since she'd grown up in a puppy mill, she needed to learn quite a few things. One of the first lessons they needed to teach her was to go to the bathroom outside. They figured that there was no way she'd be housebroken.

For the moment, however, all they cared about was taking her inside so that she could sleep off the anesthesia in the brand-new, plush, pink dog bed that Braden had run out and bought for her. They put a few dog toys next to it for when she woke up and secured the kitchen with a baby gate.

Although they weren't against crate training, they didn't want to confine this particular one to any type of cage for fear of dredging up horrifying memories.

The following day, Dixie awoke to the sound of Patricia climbing over the baby gate into the kitchen to make some coffee. The slightly confused dog slowly wagged her tail and paced the floor. Patricia took that as her cue that she needed to go out.

Much to Patricia's surprise, Dixie didn't have a single accident in the house, and it only took a few weeks to get her used to a routine of going outside at set times.

Dixie wasn't accustomed to the simple everyday noises such as the television, radio, or the rustling of a plastic bag. She jumped at every new experience and cowered at every loud noise.

Since Glenn had such an explosive temper, Dixie exercised caution in everything she did and every move she made. She wasn't familiar with having a family to call her own, although it was something she adapted to rather quickly.

The family was warm toward her. No one yelled like Glenn and Marybeth had, and when they let her outside, they always waited for her and let her back in. She had toys to play with and a comfortable bed to sleep in. Though her fears had not yet fully subsided, she was starting to trust again, just like she did when she was a puppy.

Her thoughts of contentment always retreated to her first love, the woman who showed her how the gentleness of a human's touch should feel. Had it not been for her, she might have never warmed up to anyone.

Glenn's harsh treatment had taught her lessons no one should have to learn or endure. Even his greedy wife had been quick to wag her venomous tongue, so it was safe to say that the only acts of kindness the dog ever received were during the first six months of her life.

As the weeks went by, Dixie and Nathan's relationship developed into a partnership made in heaven. Each watched out for and consciously waited for the other before leaving a room. Dixie even slept underneath Nathan's "big boy bed," as he called it. At first, Nathan's parents wouldn't allow it, but Dixie was smart enough to pry open the door once everyone was fast asleep, and Nathan never revealed their secret.

Dixie welcomed Nathan more than most. He always smelled like candy, and his fingers tasted sweet or salty, depending on what he'd been eating that day. She also loved the fact that he always shared his animal crackers with her when no one was looking.

It was evident that Nathan might be the one person who would be able to successfully change Dixie's soured taste of humans.

Chapter 15: Harsh Reality

How do you give up the one you love and explain to her if she can't ask questions?

Weeks turned into months, and Dixie and Nathan grew closer with each day that passed. Dixie's disposition and trust improved. But Nathan's breathing became noticeably more impaired. During the night, he wheezed continuously, and when he played with Dixie, he often succumbed to uncontrollable coughing fits.

At first, Patricia and Braden thought it might only be the dander on Dixie's fur, but even after they bathed her, Nathan's condition worsened.

The doctor warned them that a dog could cause Nathan to suffer more, and until they found out the cause of his issues, it wouldn't be the best thing for him.

During his most recent checkup, the pulse oximeter had revealed that Nathan's blood oxygen level was at 68 percent. Anything under 80 was considered dangerous, especially for someone his age. The news was devastating, as the entire family, particularly Nathan, had grown attached to Dixie, and she was becoming increasingly attached to them. She had finally showed signs of trust and didn't cower at every little thing. She absolutely adored Nathan, as he did her.

Patricia and Braden wanted nothing more than to keep Dixie, so they got a second opinion on Nathan's condition. The second doctor offered the same grim advice. They had no other options. Dixie had to go, and Nathan required advanced treatment, possibly even a hospital stay.

Both Patricia and Braden thumbed through their contacts and posted messages on their social media walls for anyone who'd be willing and able to provide Dixie with a stable and loving home. The thought of surrendering her to a shelter felt like a knife piercing their hearts, so they explored every possible avenue.

But each avenue was blocked by a series of obstacles. While most people they asked showed compassion, no one was able to take in a new dog. Even the local animal rescue groups were completely full.

As a last resort, they called Dr. Fredericks. She'd been monitoring Dixie's progress since they had adopted her, so she was quite familiar with the family as well as Nathan's condition.

Patricia made the call, swallowing the lump that had taken permanent residence in her throat. "Dr. Fredericks, this is Patricia." They exchanged pleasantries before she continued. "As you know, Nathan has been suffering with respiratory issues, and the doctors don't know the cause. They've advised us, however, that since we've adopted Dixie, he's gotten much worse. They feel that the dog could be hindering his progress."

Dr. Fredericks listened sympathetically as Patricia continued. "Is there any way possible, in your line of work, that you'd happen to know anyone willing to adopt her? This poor dog has been through enough and was just gaining confidence. It breaks my heart to have to do this. I want...no, I *need* her to go to a good family. I just can't bear the thought of her enduring any more pain and disappointment."

After contemplating the situation for a moment, Dr. Fredericks promised to offer as much help as she could. "I can't think of anyone offhand, but give me a few hours, possibly a day. Let me make a few phone calls to other veterinarians around town. They may be able to get the word out."

"Thank you so much, doc. Please, anything you can do would be greatly appreciated."

"I understand completely. I'll be in touch. The last thing I want is to see Dixie suffer."

As Patricia hung up the phone, a river of tears streamed down her face. She looked at her innocent dog staring back at her with her light-brown eyes. And Dixie knew that something was amiss. Patricia bent down, sat on the tile floor, and cradled Dixie's small face in her hands while she kissed her velvety ears. "I'm so sorry, baby. I'd keep you if I could." The gentle dog licked her face, cleaning each and every teardrop that fell.

Then, instinctively, she picked up her favorite toy and nestled her body closer to Patricia before sitting in her lap. Patricia hugged her close and didn't want to let go. By the time she got up, the dog's fur was drenched with her tears. Dixie's trusting eyes stared deeply into her own.

Patricia prayed for the phone to ring with good news. There was no way she could send Dixie back to a shelter.

Chapter 16: Planting the Seed

Just when you think you don't make a difference in someone's life, you may be the one person who does.

Jerry and his pals met up at the local buffet, each showing up on their motorcycle of choice. Jerry's was a Boulevard, while the rest of his friends were brand loyal to their Harleys.

The four of them had been best friends since junior high school and supported each other in whatever venture they were planning, issue they were resolving, or decision they were making. When they heard the horrid story of the puppy mill, each did more than just support Jerry—they made it their issue too. After all, they all loved dogs, each more than the next.

Kyle was a police officer, Dave was a lawyer, Peter was a certified black belt and trainer at Master Yen's Karate, and Jerry was an ex-Marine who owned his own business as a mechanic.

Four determined, muscular men on a mission. Good news for the dogs. Not so good news for Glenn.

Jerry described the situation to each of his buddies over a couple of mimosas and omelets. Their muscles flexed when they heard the dire circumstances that the dogs had to tolerate. Other than Jerry, none of the men had even *seen* the mill yet.

Kyle had the most experience with these types of people, as at one point during his tenure he had worked in the department of animal control at the precinct. He knew all too much about backyard breeders and puppy mills, and he had his fair share of frustration with trying to shut them down.

Kyle told the men that most puppy mill owners know the law as it pertains to them and know how to avoid getting caught. Few of them ever go down without a fight. But Jerry laughed and took it all in stride, as Glenn would be no match for the four of them. If the law wouldn't stop him, they would.

The fact that Jerry knew Glenn personally was a big advantage, especially since Glenn also owned the puppy store that sold the dogs. It was under his wife's name—a minor technicality. By the time they finished breakfast, they'd already outlined a decent plan and could hardly wait to implement it.

Though they agreed that they might have to break a few minor laws in the process, they were ready to start their mission to bring disaster to Glenn and his beautiful wife.

Chapter 17: Never Give Up

Have faith. Things might work out better than expected.

Dr. Fredericks took a little longer than expected to call back, but it was well worth the wait. Her resourcefulness proved to be a reliable asset as she got in touch with an old colleague and classmate from college, Dr. Louise Hill. In grim situations like these, dog lovers always band together and do their best to find a means to an end.

When Dr. Fredericks described the lamentable situation to her, Dr. Hill recalled one of her clients coming into her office a couple of years prior with a pregnant Nova Scotia duck toller. It was easy to recall that breed, because they were extremely rare in Las Vegas. She couldn't help but wonder if Dixie could be one of the pups—then chuckled at the irony when she discovered the name on the microchip. In life, sometimes lucky coincidences do happen. Indeed, she had a match. She then contemplated whether Chelsea and Anthony would be interested.

Though she didn't see them frequently, they visited annually when Sugar and Spice came in for their checkups. It had been almost a year since she'd last seen them.

As soon as the clock chimed nine, Dr. Hill picked up the phone, crossed her fingers, and dialed their number.

"Hello," a female voice answered.

"Good morning, is this Chelsea?" In the background, a baby was crying.

"Yes, who's speaking please?"

"Chelsea, it's Dr. Hill. Did I catch you at a bad time?"

"No, not at all. I was just laying Emma down for a nap."

Uncertain of who Emma was, Dr. Hill paused but didn't ask any questions. She knew Chelsea and Anthony had previously tried to conceive, but the cards had previously been stacked against them. She didn't want to say anything inappropriate. They might have only been babysitting.

"Oh, my gosh, that's right," Chelsea said. "I haven't spoken to you in almost a year. Emma is our new daughter. She's three month's old now. The doctors weren't correct after all!"

"Wow, that's fantastic, Chelsea! Congratulations." Dr. Hill was truly happy for them, but she couldn't help but feel somewhat defeated as she thought they'd never want to handle both a newborn and a new dog. She contemplated just forgetting the whole thing, but figured she had nothing to lose since she already had her on the phone.

"Chelsea, I have something to ask you. Actually it's the reason I'm calling."

"Sure, is everything okay?"

"Well, yes, but a colleague of mine notified me that one of her clients had found a stray dog roaming the streets. When we scanned her for a microchip, your phone number and the dog's name, Foxy, came up. I assume your husband must have given her the number of the people that had purchased her?"

"Yes, that's correct. I do remember him telling me about that. I was thankful that she was found unharmed. That puppy had formed a tight grip on my heartstrings."

"Well, unfortunately, what wasn't told to your husband was that she wasn't exactly in top health. It appeared that she was living in a puppy mill. When she was found, the collar around her neck was nothing more than a sharp piece of metal with an ID number on it."

Chelsea caught her breath as the veterinarian continued. Memories came flooding back of the adorable puppy that she loved and lost.

"I don't want you to worry as she is fine now," Dr. Fredericks said. "A nice family picked her up, but as I said, she was previously living in a puppy mill and was in terrible shape when they found her.

"Unfortunately, the family that adopted her has a young boy with some health issues, and though the dog has grown quite attached, they've been advised by doctors to surrender the dog. I realize this comes at a bad time, but..." She hesitated, hoping that this story would have a happy ending. "Would you have any interest in adopting?"

There was nothing but silence on the other end of the phone, and Dr. Hill interpreted that as a no. "I apologize. I shouldn't have called. I normally don't get involved—"

"No! I'm glad you called. I'm sorry. I'm just devastated to hear what she's been through. I had no idea. I don't know what to say."

"I understand. It's okay. I'll try a few more people. I'm sorry to bother you."

"No, please! Please. I just have to think this through. Yeah, we have our hands full with Sugar and Spice and now Emma, but I can't allow Foxy to go through any more trauma. You have to understand how much I loved that puppy. It sickened me to let her go and now it makes my blood curdle to know I sold her to a puppy mill of all places. I remember that day like it was yesterday. I had no idea they ran a puppy mill. That couple acted like such charmers."

"They usually do. She was in pretty bad shape, so I've been told. My old colleague, Dr. Fredericks, has been monitoring her progress ever since the family took her in.

She said she is much healthier now and has been in good hands."

"Where is she now?"

"She is still with her new family. They are grief-stricken. The young boy and she became fast friends. They renamed her Dixie."

Again Chelsea fell silent as she contemplated, but only for a moment. "I have to talk to Anthony." She hesitated again, knowing she had some convincing to do and knowing full well that she'd be in over her head. "I think I can convince him, but it's only fair that I talk this over with him first."

"I completely understand. When should I check back with you?"

"Would tomorrow morning be okay? He gets home around dinnertime. I want to make sure he's in the right frame of mind before I spring this on him."

"Absolutely. I'll call you tomorrow. I'll also give you my cell phone in case you need to call me before then."

Dr. Hill crossed her fingers and gave Dr. Fredericks a call, who in turn called Patricia.

Patricia had been pacing the floor, waiting by the phone all day just praying for good news. Though this call wasn't a confirmation of a silver lining, it was far better than she'd expected.

As Patricia hung up with the doctor, she hugged Dixie once again and tried to occupy her time until the next day. She wanted to remain hopeful, but she realized it was quite possible that the answer may be no. She wracked her brain for another viable candidate, but again, none came to mind.

Chapter 18: Above the Law?

You'd be amazed at what you can accomplish with a little help from your friends.

While Glenn happily went about his daily macabre business of mating malnourished dogs with lively profit-inducing studs, Jerry and his pals were busy following through with their plan to make sure that Glenn's escapades came to a screeching halt.

While two in the group were law-abiding citizens, Jerry and Peter were not averse to bending a rule or two to get the job done once and for all. They hoped it didn't have to come to that, and Kyle and Dave smirked as they promised to look the other way. They knew their buddies wouldn't do anything that would compromise their careers. If they did, Jerry and Peter had no problem taking the heat. After all, it was for a good cause.

Since he was an officer of the law, Kyle had access to dozens of records and rap sheets for convicted criminals. While he had some time alone at the station, he browsed through them for a Mr. Glenn and Mrs. Marybeth Kennedy. He expected them to be in their database for at least a traffic ticket or two, but never expected to find such a large basket of dirty laundry, plus a full bucket of outstanding warrants.

The list started when Glenn was in his teens and included burglary, identity theft, DWIs, hit and run, possession of an illegal substance, domestic abuse to his ex-wife, and a host of other violations. It was a wonder that he hadn't been thrown in jail years ago.

While Marybeth had a cleaner record than Glenn, she was no angel herself. She also had her fair share of convictions, including drug usage, DWIs, and even prostitution.

While Kyle didn't find anything in the records yet that could incriminate Glenn enough for him to go to jail forever, he could easily intimidate Glenn and dig a little deeper. He smiled as he conjured up ways to make Glenn sweat. Among the rest of his skills, Kyle was an effective interrogator. He was above average in intelligence and had mastered the ability to make any suspect paranoid. That was a role he played flawlessly.

Dave, as an attorney, searched for every loophole that might put Glenn and his wife out of business. Since the mill was effectively in their own backyard, they were already in violation of zoning laws. There was a fine line between backyard breeders and puppy mills, but either way, they hadn't registered their dogs and hadn't given them proper care. If they had over fifty dogs, that was another violation.

He checked with his buddy that worked for the city to find out if a pet fancier's permit had ever been received by them. No. That simple fifty-dollar permit had never been applied for, most likely because Glenn didn't want to draw attention to his already tainted name. Another violation. Dave was certain there were plenty more where that came from. And those applied only to the mill. His next course of action was to check out the store. He was confident he'd find unhealthy conditions for the pups there.

Having known Dr. Hill for quite some time, he stopped by her office for advice on what to look for to prove poor health in puppies. The information she provided was priceless.

The rest of his afternoon was spent inside Playful Pups Puppy Shop, looking for telltale signs. And sure enough, he didn't have to look far. One of the pups was coughing nonstop, a sure sign of kennel cough. The cages were undeniably filthy. In another cage, one of the pups was violently scratching at their ears, indicating ear mites.

Just as he was about to walk out, an irate woman walked in and marched toward Marybeth. She began screaming, and Dave had to stick around to find out what all of the commotion was about. "I called you five times. Five times! You refused to take my phone calls. The puppy you sold me not only has ear mites, but worms and kennel cough. What kind of place are you running?"

Marybeth pretended she'd never received the messages. "I'm sorry; my staff must've forgotten to tell me that you called. I'd be happy to exchange the puppy for you."

"Exchange it? Did you just say you'd exchange the puppy? What is she, a ripped sweater? She's a living, breathing thing. We're not going to exchange her. Are you out of your mind?"

"Well, what I mean is, we'd be happy to give you one that is healthy. I can take the sick one off your hands, and you can have your choice of the puppies in the cage over there." She pointed to a pen of pups of the same breed, which only infuriated the woman more.

"I can't believe what I'm hearing. You can't be serious. Please tell me that you have a warped sense of humor and this is your idea of a sick joke. Exchange a dog? Is that how you rectify things? Exchange the puppies and then what? Kill the sick ones? I should've known how shady you were when you didn't have papers showing her ancestry lines. You were going to charge me two hundred for those. I've checked around; those papers should be free if you're legit."

"Ma'am, I assure you—" The woman cut her off, looking like she wanted nothing more than to knock her out right then and there. "You're buying your puppies from a mill, aren't you? You're not getting them from a breeder. Keep your money. I would never exchange my dog. I hope you rot in hell."

Dave had never wanted to give a standing ovation so much in his life. She deserved a medal for sticking it to Marybeth. All of the other customers heard the shouting and slowly eased their way toward the front door. At least for the hour, profits would be down for Marybeth and Glenn.

The woman turned on her heel and stormed out, kicking the front door open as she left. Dave wished that the glass had fallen out of it.

The scene enraged him as well, and this was only the start. He knew that once he got up close and personal with the puppy mill, he was going to be further outraged. Seeing all of those dogs suffering might spark a flame that no amount of water could extinguish.

Jerry and Peter planned to be there when the shit hit the fan to provide strength and backup. Should Glenn decide to get out of hand, either of them would be able to knock him off his feet without batting an eye.

The other parts of the plan that involved Jerry and Peter were risky, but the potential reward was far greater than the risk.

Dave smiled and looked straight at Marybeth as she counted money in the cash register, trying to act like nothing had happened.

His first thought was *This is going to be fun.*

Chapter 19: Absolute Glee

Some of the best things in life don't cost a dime. Rescuing an animal is one of them.

By the time Anthony had arrived home, Emma was sleeping as most newborns do, and Sugar and Spice were on their best behavior. Chelsea had jokingly briefed them to behave themselves when Anthony got home, and coincidentally they obliged.

When he walked in the door, he had a feeling that something was up. It was true that they generally had a great marriage, but on this particular evening, Chelsea went out of her way to make her husband comfortable, including cooking a full meal and opening a new bottle of his favorite wine. Scented candles added to the tranquil ambiance, which she hoped would put him in a relaxed and obliging mood. She knew well in advance that convincing him was going to take some work.

"Wine? It's not even Friday yet."

"So?" She smirked as she took a sip. "I have nine months of drinking to make up for, so I figured tonight was as good a night as any."

"Uh-huh. Why aren't I buying that story? Now, tell me what's really up." There were times when it frustrated her that he knew her so well. "I've known you too long not to know when you're lying. The way you curl your hair through your fingers is a dead giveaway. Yep, just like that, and the way you shift in your chair like you just did. Time to fess up." He was half afraid of what she might divulge to him and half amused at the way she was going about it. He had to admit, so far, he was enjoying the show.

"Well, I got a call today."

"Yep."

"And, it was from Dr. Hill."

"Really? Dr. Hill? Is everything okay?"

"Yeah, well…yeah, kinda." She wanted to kick herself; she felt she needed to have more confidence and be convincing.

He cocked his head to demonstrate that he was listening and to encourage her to go on. He still couldn't figure out where she was going with this.

"Remember those puppies we had?"

Mindful now of where the story might lead, he nodded.

"Well, remember the last one we sold?"

He laughed. As if he could ever forget. His wife had cried for days after she left.

"You mean Foxy?"

Taken aback that he knew her name, she asked, "You knew?"

"That you named the dog? Of course I did! Didn't you think I heard you every time you sneaked down the stairs in the middle of the night to snuggle with her? I suppose you didn't know that I heard you singing to her, did you?"

She couldn't help but smile. All this time she thought she put on a good display like she was a pillar of strength, when her husband was onto her the whole time. She should've known he could see right through her.

He smiled softly at her. "So, what about Foxy?"

"Well, Dr. Hill said she was found roaming the streets."

"I remember. I got that phone call and gave them Glenn Kennedy's number, remember?"

"Well, yeah, but Glenn wasn't the honorable family man he had boasted about. Another family found her and had adopted her that same day that you received the call."

"Wow, really? Is she okay?" Though he was a little more reserved than his wife, Anthony really did love all of the pups. He also knew he had to be the logical one from time to time, as his wife would've kept all of them if it were up to her. He hated to hear that the dog had been wandering all alone.

"She's okay now, but the kicker is that those awful people we sold her to were running a puppy mill, and that is where Foxy lived for the past year. When they found her, she was in horrible shape. She was malnourished, her hair was matted, and what kills me is that she was scared. That puppy had nothing but confidence when she lived here. They said a metal collar was wrapped so tight around her neck that it cut into her skin. They had to cut it off with clippers. The family that adopted her fell in love with her, but their son has a serious medical condition. They can't keep her any longer."

Anthony nodded sympathetically. He didn't need for his wife to continue. He knew her well enough to know what she was going to ask. "And Dr. Hill called you." He said, rather than asked.

"Yes. She wanted to know if—"

"We could adopt her."

Chelsea nodded, knowing what her husband was thinking, but was determined to make him see her point.

"So, what do you want to do?"

She was surprised that he even asked, and her eyes lit up. "Well, I know we have our hands full, but I say we go get her."

"Of course you'd say that. You do realize we have a newborn sleeping in the other room, don't you?"

Chelsea raised her guard just a little, stiffened her back, and nodded. "What's one more dog?" She knew in her heart she could handle another dog, even if it would be a lot more work.

Anthony couldn't help but smirk. She was good. He knew her unfaltering mind was already made up, and nothing he said was going to change it, but he still had to give her a hard time. He enjoyed toying with her just enough to get her going.

"What if the dog isn't good with kids? What if she tries to bite Emma? Then what?"

"She *is* good with kids. That's the best part. Their son was only three when they met, and she is wonderful with him. They became the best of friends. We can see for ourselves."

"And you can handle taking care of a newborn and three dogs?

She waved her hand at him. "Sugar and Spice are already trained. As a matter of fact, Spice has learned to fetch me a clean diaper when I need one. He's quite the little helper. And Sugar lets me know when Emma is fussing in her crib. I don't even need those baby monitors. What's one more dog? I'm sure she's housebroken by now, and we've already agreed that I am quitting my job in another two weeks. That'll give me plenty of time to be a stay-at-home mom and dog trainer. Foxy, or Dixie as they now call her, will be the model citizen in no time."

"Dixie? Is that her name now?" He smirked as his wife face turned crimson.

"Yes." She fussed with the tablecloth and took another swig of wine. She figured she'd need it at this rate.

"You sound convinced. Am I right?"

"Well, I don't see the harm in another dog. We have a big enough house, a big enough yard, and frankly we do okay financially."

Going in for the kill, he got up, walked over to his wife, stood behind her, and gently massaged her shoulders. He felt how tense she was and decided he had to stop playing his game. He leaned down and kissed her on the cheek. As he did, he whispered, "You're crazy, you know that? You have this mindset that you can save the world. But I love you for your outrageously big and goofy heart. Your damn heart overpowers your brain sometimes, and all logic flies out the window like dust in a windstorm, but there's no one in this world more committed to dogs than you."

Chelsea looked up at her husband, still holding her determined stare, but then softening it just a bit, waiting to hear her husband's response. Her hand remained on the wine glass just in case this was going to be an all-night discussion.

"Gosh," he said. "You got me. I'd be a fool if I didn't condone adopting Foxy—or Dixie, or whatever her name is. Of course we'll make it work." He turned so that he was now facing his wife and looking in her eyes. "When can we get her?"

Tears leaked out of the corners of Chelsea's eyes and she got up and threw her arms around Anthony. She remembered the reason she loved her husband so much, as he was the one person who understood her uncontrollable urge to save as many dogs as humanly possible.

Once the tears ceased, a broad smile formed on her face, and she answered him, "How's nine tomorrow. Can you go into work late?"

"I can do better than that. That poor dog deserves a proper homecoming, including a new bed, new toys, and a couple of fancy bones. I'm taking the day off."

Chapter 20: Calculated Plans

Isn't it funny how everything worthwhile seems unattainable until you take your first step? You find that light at the end of the tunnel only gets brighter as you get closer to your goal.

Dave and Jerry got together with Kyle and Pete to disclose their findings. Unable to contain his excitement, Dave was the first one to boast. "I feel very confident that we've gotten ourselves a case. I walked into that pet store and wanted nothing more than to turn around and walk right out. If Marybeth was a man, I would've punched him in the nose. Get this; they don't even have a pet fancier's permit for their lot. That right there is a huge violation.

"Do we know how many dogs they are housing back there? Is it over fifty, Jerry?"

"There's gotta be more than that. I was only in that yard for an hour at most, and I quickly surveyed it the best I could. But, yeah, it's safe to say that there are a lot of dogs. They have one of the biggest lots in Vegas. No wonder they can run a puppy mill right behind their own house."

Peter was curious now. "Don't the neighbors hear anything? Smell anything? No one's ever complained?"

"They live on a four-acre lot. It's probably the only one in this town. There's plenty of room to hide whatever they want, and there's plenty of space between homes. I'm sure they paid a pretty penny for that much land. It's quite possible no one even knows." Jerry had to admit it did seem that someone would have complained at one point in time.

Kyle confirmed it for them. "Oh, no, some people complained under the identity of anonymous. We don't know if it was a neighbor or just a concerned person who passed by the house, but there have been numerous complaints. He circumvented the system somehow, but those complaints are still on the computer. I might be able to add a few more." He winked at his buddies. "A few white lies never hurt anybody, except for Glenn and his lovely wife, that is."

Then Kyle added, "They both have rap sheets miles long. Did you know that Marybeth was a prostitute?"

"Doesn't surprise me," Jerry said. "The day I took Bentley to her house, she was cursing like a truck driver who just hit a shit load of traffic. Takes a special kinda lady to talk like that."

"Jerry, I'm especially thankful that you didn't go through with the breeding. Poor Bentley must've been terrified."

"Nah, he was none the wiser. I'm not sure I'll get over it though. That's why we have to make this work. What's the plan, Kyle?"

"Well, when I go to the station, I'm going to go through his long list of complaints with a fine-toothed comb. I'll give animal control a reason to check it out. Since they don't have a pet fancier's permit, that's strike one right there. If they have more than fifty dogs, that's strike two. Harsh living conditions, Jerry, can you confirm that?"

"Definitely, I saw a dog in a cage that was missing fur down the middle of her back and on her legs. Poor thing. I still can't believe that Glenn convinced me that he was a breeder."

"Okay, so harsh living conditions, strike three. The health of the dogs, strike four."

Dave added, "Oh, let's not forget, their home is almost in foreclosure. Damn fools buying a house like that when they can't even afford it. If we charge them with enough fines, it's quite feasible they can lose their home. Any traffic tickets, Kyle?"

"Two, unpaid. I have a few friends who can make sure they get a few more."

"Yeah, and I can bust their taillights on their cars to add to those violations." Pete laughed as he said it, though they all knew he was dead serious. He was the rebel of the group, but he always had his heart in the right place, even if some of the things he did were against the law.

"So, off the bat, we've got four strikes against them, plus some beefed up traffic violations, right?" Jerry asked.

"Sounds about right," Peter said. "Hell, I really have nothing to lose. I may bust a few things around their house too. Don't worry, nothing major, but enough damage to cause them to have to shell out more money."

"Well, summer's around the corner," Jerry said. "When I was over there, I noticed that their air-conditioner is on the ground. From what I understand, it costs at least eight thousand per unit for each floor. They have two."

Peter smiled. "Ah, now you're thinking, Jerry. Thanks for the tip. I can make sure it just simply stops working."

They all laughed at that. Pete was right. He didn't have anything to lose. If he got caught vandalizing their property, he had enough money to bail himself out of jail.

"Besides, if I get locked up, I know a good lawyer, right, Dave?"

"You sure do. I got your back, buddy. Don't worry about it." Of course, they all hoped it wouldn't have to come to that.

The group was getting excited. They knew how difficult it was to shut down a puppy mill, and they knew they might have to break a few laws to get the results they desired and prevent Glenn and Marybeth from ever opening another puppy mill again. Aside from killing them both, which was out of the question, this was the only plausible way.

"Hey, guys," Jerry said. "I just want to say thank you. I know you are all putting your careers—not to mention your lives—on the line, so if at any time you feel you can't go through with this, I'll understand."

"No way, Jerry," Kyle said. "We're in this for the long haul, right guys? And the way it looks now, we might not have to do anything. They did a pretty decent job of digging their own graves."

Dave and Pete eagerly agreed.

Kyle was a dog lover who owned three dogs himself —a German shepherd, a Bernese mountain dog, and a Yorkie. He'd been on a silent crusade against puppy mills ever since they first appeared on the map and wanted to do what he could to close them down. "It's worth it. We're not doing anything really bad. We're just enhancing the violations they've already committed. And Pete might have to regress to his youth by adding some vandalism. You have enough experience with that, don't ya, Pete?" Pete faked a dirty look. "In all seriousness though, those dogs are worth every minute of it."

Dave brought up another valid point. "Let's not forget that we need to shut down the puppy store. Without their own puppy mill, it would be difficult to operate, but not impossible. They can always find another mill; there's thousands." The group listened and nodded in agreement as he continued on. "I've got the health inspector going there this afternoon. I can only imagine what he'll find. We'll put these two on the streets, literally, and quite frankly, they deserve to experience every ounce of pain and heartache that those dogs have gone through. Kyle, how soon can animal control be there?"

"Let me have a look at those 'files' we spoke of, then I'll call animal control. Tomorrow afternoon, at the latest."

"And the traffic violations?"

"Easy. I'll have a rookie follow Marybeth on her way home from the shop. She'll have a nice, shiny new ticket by the time she walks through the front door of her magnificent home."

"Yeah, and it looks like I have some vandalism to do tonight," Peter added. "I'm going to have to dig through my tools to find one that can bust compressors on air-conditioning units." They all shared a good laugh and couldn't wait to get the ball rolling.

"Talk about having a bad day," Kyle said. "They're going to have a bad rest of their lives."

Chapter 21: The Meaning of Perfect

Every now and then, the stars align properly, and you are given the opportunity for a second chance. Seize it with open arms.

Chelsea was over the moon and enormously relieved. Not wanting to waste any more precious time, she phoned Dr. Hill on her cell phone without hesitation so the message could be relayed to Dr. Fredericks and the appointment could be arranged. When the doctor answered, Chelsea could hardly contain her excitement. "Tell them yes. I'll pick her up tomorrow."

"Really?!" The vet exclaimed. "Are you sure?"

Chelsea laughed. "No, not at all, but close enough. Anthony is doing his best not to flip his lid, and I'm sure he's convinced I'm crazy. The truth is that I never stopped thinking of that dog, and my heart cringes when I realize what happened to her. Please give me the address, and tell them we can be there at nine."

"That's so exciting, Chelsea! I will call Dr. Fredericks and have her set the whole thing up."

"Thanks so much for thinking of me, Dr. Hill. I can't tell you how much I appreciate it."

"You're welcome, and thank you! I can't wait to share the good news. This is a nice change from how this type of situation often turn out."

When they hung up, Dr. Hill wasted no time in calling Dr. Fredericks. As she had mentioned to Chelsea, it was refreshing to hear happy endings instead of what she saw come into her office every now and then. Quite often, people disposed of dogs like yesterday's garbage, not caring about the dog's well-being or where it would wind up.

When she saw people who actually cared, it reminded her why she went into the veterinary field in the first place.

"Good news, Tracy!"

"Please tell me. They'll take her?"

"Yes! She wants to set up a time to meet the family tomorrow. She'd like to be there at nine."

"That's fantastic! I'll let them know, and I'm sure it won't be a problem."

"Okay, here's her phone number. Her name is Chelsea. She was the one who sold the dog to the puppy mill—unknowingly, of course."

"That is incredible. What a twist of fate! Thank you so much. I'll be in touch."

Dr. Fredericks acted as the liaison between Chelsea and Patricia and set up their meeting. While Patricia was still distraught, a heavy weight lifted off her shoulders when she learned who was going to adopt Dixie. Things had gone full circle; Dixie was going where she belonged.

Chapter 22: Reunited

It's not a coincidence that when you rescue the life of another, you often rescue your own as well.

As expected, Chelsea hardly slept during the night, as she couldn't contain her excitement. Slightly concerned about how she would handle both a newborn and a new dog, she spent the evening thinking of every possible obstacle and countered it with a viable solution.

When she rolled out of bed bright and early the following morning, she brewed a fresh pot of Irish Cream flavored coffee and ran to the store to get bagels. Even without sleep, she felt more refreshed than she had in a long time.

Anthony stumbled down the stairs when she got home and laughed at his overzealous wife. "I'd say someone is in a good mood. You were tossing and turning all night, so how is it that you are so full of energy?"

She looked into her husband's eyes and flashed a smile. "I did toss and turn. I spent all night trying to convince myself this is a bad idea. And guess what? I couldn't think of one reason, hence the reason for my good mood. I've never felt more certain about anything in my life. I'm thoroughly convinced—it's karma. It was meant to be." She kissed him good morning and reached over to pour him a cup of coffee.

"Karma, huh? You're not going to be getting all spiritual now, are you?" he teased.

"Call it what you will. Foxy was meant to be ours."

"Her name is Dixie now, lest you forget."

"Her name is going to be Foxy again. She'll remember. Trust me. We had a bond."

"Oh, believe me, I already know that. You thought you were so sly. I couldn't believe when you actually let that couple in the house to buy her. I'm surprised you didn't bury them out in the backyard along with your dead parakeet."

"Believe me, if I knew then what I know now, they would be buried. Despicable people. And I never had a parakeet."

Anthony chuckled. "Oh, must've been my other wife." He laughed. "Okay, killer wife, don't go getting any more brilliant ideas about burying people. It's almost time to go, isn't it?"

"Yes! We can take my car."

"Ohhh, no. You're way too excited. We'll take my truck over there."

Chelsea smiled. He was right. "Sure. Let's go!"

As they drove over, they realized they lived closer than they thought. They arrived fifteen minutes early, but Patricia and her family were sitting on the front lawn playing with Dixie. Before the truck even came to a full stop, Chelsea had her hand on the door handle.

Anthony could only laugh at his enthusiastic wife. He worried that she'd catapult out the door before he even applied the brakes.

He stopped the truck, jumped out, and walked over to her side of the truck. As he removed Emma from her car seat, Chelsea got out and stood there a minute to get a good look at the dog. She couldn't believe how much she had grown and how closely she resembled both Sugar and Spice. Her eyes were still as beautiful as she remembered, and her puffy cheeks had slimmed down just a bit. At that moment, Chelsea realized just how much she missed her and regretted letting her go. But now, things were going to be as they were meant to be.

Dixie looked up at the truck. She'd recognize that scent anywhere. She saw Chelsea step out and remembered the wonderful woman immediately. The same woman who showed her nothing but kindness and love. The woman who used to bring her little toys and treats. The woman who used to sneak downstairs in the middle of the night to snuggle with her, to kiss her on the head, and to find the tickle spot on her tummy.

Dixie's ears perked up, and her face displayed surprise and utter joy, her eyes were wide, and her tail wagged with enthusiasm.

It was as if Dixie had been given the strength of a buffalo as she broke the leash handle in two and escaped from Patricia's grasp. With obvious merriment that can only be born from seeing one's true love, Dixie darted across the desert landscape and over to her previous owner.

Before Chelsea could bend down to hug her, Dixie jumped into her arms, smothering her lips and watering eyes with dozens of slimy kisses. Her tail wagged nonstop as she whined with uninhibited jubilation. Full of excitement, Dixie even nibbled on Chelsea's chin a bit.

Patricia and her family broke into a sea of tears, and even Anthony couldn't build a dam strong enough to hold back the waterworks. Through euphoric sobs, Chelsea blurted out, "She remembers me." She tried to wipe the tears from her eyes, but as soon as she did, another steady stream leaked out. "Foxy!"

Chapter 23: Progress

Determination is a word used lightly, but when exercised properly, it achieves amazing results.

The determined assemblage of the four men, who now proudly referred to themselves as "The Rescuers," set out to accomplish what they promised they would.

Peter felt a smidge of sympathy as he realized that they were really going to ruin the Kennedy's lives. That irrational feeling quickly passed.

He had taken a survey of the property the night before to make sure they knew where all the entrances to the backyard were. He was quick, efficient, and ninja-like in his ability to remain undetected.

He was elated that soon they would even the score, since Glenn had lied outright to Jerry and almost pulled Jerry into his nefarious lifestyle of torturing puppies and female dogs. God only knows what would've happened to Bentley if Jerry had left him in Glenn's care for a full week.

The health inspector that Dave had hired came through for them in more ways than one. He determined that the puppy shop was not up to code by any means and that the owners had broken a multitude of laws. The puppies were not only sick but also terribly undernourished. Their cages were revolting, and high on the list of offenses was the fact that not one of the pups had been given the required shots. The scene at the store could only be labeled as horrendous.

Dave also advised the group that while Glenn and Marybeth both had a steady source of income right now, they didn't always. As a result, they had accumulated hundreds of thousands in debt. It was likely impossible for them to pay it off. They were way behind on mortgage payments on the house; the bank was about to start foreclosure proceedings within the next three weeks if the Kennedy's didn't pay over twenty thousand dollars for missed payments.

The pet shop was short in its rent by over four months. The landlord told Dave when he pretended that he needed a credit reference that she was ready to evict Glenn and Marybeth any day.

They were up shit creek without a paddle, and yet they went about their daily business as if nothing was awry. They had no idea that The Rescuers were pulling every string possible to expedite their financial demise.

As it turned out, sabotaging their property was unnecessary. Kyle added a few more recent open tickets to the computer, just for extra padding, and he was confident that no one would know who was behind it. If they did, it was likely that no one would care.

A summons would then be served to Glenn, and he'd have no choice but to appear in court. He had enough traffic tickets to cause him to lose his license—another expense he wouldn't be able to afford.

The fines, the foreclosure proceedings, and the closing of the store were plenty to put Glenn and Marybeth out of business. They would have no other choice but to surrender the dogs and give up their operation, their house, and likely even their cars.

The plan was in motion. Now it was time to sit back and let the chips fall where they may.

Chapter 24: Friends for Life

There is no truer, greater reward than the love received from a dog. It never forgets and will remain loyal to the very end.

The moment held bittersweet emotions for everyone. Sweet Foxy had been living just a few pitchforks away from the depths of hell, only to find a loving family who then had to give her up. Thankfully, it was to the one woman Foxy loved the most. Of course, as with everything in Foxy's young life, there was a price to pay. She didn't understand that she'd never get to see her best buddy, Nathan, ever again.

And Nathan didn't quite understand the level of mourning he was going to feel. Not only would he never see his dog again, but the doctors felt it necessary to put him in the hospital on Monday to monitor his lung function. They were concerned that he would need to be on a ventilator.

Chelsea felt an overpowering surge of guilt, as did Anthony secretly, for selling Foxy in the first place. She felt she should've been honest with her husband at the time instead of trying to put up a front. Because she hadn't been, Foxy had to withstand that terrible ordeal.

She wasn't able to feel down in the dumps for long, however, because Foxy was still so excited at her reclaimed love that she danced in a circle and shook her stuffed gorilla side to side putting the focus back on her.

Both families joined in an effort to give her one last happy memory of everyone she loved together in one place.

At that moment Chelsea found the answer to suppress the guilt she'd been harboring. "Patricia?"

Through sobs, Patricia tried to maintain her composure and answered, "Yes?"

"I've been thinking about your situation, and it's plain to see how much Foxy does love your family. That being said, is there any reason why we can't keep in touch? I mean, I know how much you love Foxy, well, Dixie." They both smiled at the awkwardness. "And I know that awful void of losing her all too well. It's not easy."

Patricia nodded, and Chelsea continued. "Why don't we exchange numbers and keep in touch? You can come visit her, or I can bring her here. Besides, with three dogs, we're going to need a good dog sitter—that is, if you wouldn't mind dealing with two more dogs every now and again? At my house, of course. I wouldn't want to expose Nathan to more pet dander."

Short of words and unable to speak them anyway, Patricia nodded and hugged Chelsea. Tears streamed down both of the women's faces.

Sure enough, Foxy had to split it up by showing off her healthy set of lungs and howling at them—just like Spice did the day he stole Chelsea's heart in the shelter.

Chapter 25: Closer

Follow your dreams to the end. If you quit too soon, you might've missed out on the pot of gold waiting right around the corner.

The Rescuers' plan moved forward.

Dave fueled the spreading fire with the shop's landlord, hinting that he thought Glenn and Marybeth were drug pushers, using the shop as a way to scout out customers. That was all that the paranoid landlord needed to hear.

Previously, her husband had managed all the properties, but since he'd passed away the year before, she didn't put up with any funny business. If any of her tenants were drug pushers, in addition to being consistently late on their rent, they were as good as gone in her book.

While portions of their plan would've been comical if the situation weren't so dire, other aspects were downright awful. Jerry and Peter watched in awe as animal control surveyed the Kennedy's backyard. Glenn and Marybeth were taken by surprise but had no choice but to let the inspectors do their job.

The atrocious scene that unraveled was horrifying. Dogs missing fur from various parts of their bodies, infections in their eyes, spinal problems, mange. The astounding list of ailments was endless.

A few of the bigger dogs had been suffering in a small crate for so long that they could no longer stand up. Others had broken legs that looked as though they might never heal properly. Those that didn't have broken bones were obviously malnourished; the outlines of their rib cages protruded from their scrawny bodies.

The fur on some was so long that it dangled in front of their tear-encrusted eyes. Each case seemed to be worse than the last.

Both Dr. Hill and Dr. Fredericks had been called. Jerry warned them that there would be at least fifty dogs in need of examinations, if not more. It was conceivable that some would not even make it.

Glenn and Marybeth weren't going down without a fight, though both of them secretly knew they had no chance at winning. While animal control was allowed to give the average person leniency to get a dog fanciers permit and a zoning permit for breeding animals, the scene there simply violated too many codes. The enormous level of neglect and the various counts of animal cruelty would crush them in a court of law, and they knew it.

Toward the end of the visit, both Glenn and Marybeth surrendered to animal control, allowing them to remove the animals from the premises. They swore to anyone that would listen that they'd be pressing charges. As most of the officers on site were clearly disgusted, no one paid them the slightest bit of attention. The day that they'd be able to afford a lawyer would be the day cows really did fly over the moon.

Jerry stood on the sidelines and watched, anxious to bring the couple down and wondering if Glenn and Marybeth knew who was responsible for their own downfall. Perhaps most importantly, he wondered if Glenn and Marybeth felt one ounce of remorse.

He shook his head. He was certain the answer was *no*.

Hours later, once all the dogs were removed from the mill and the shop, the arresting officers arrived on scene to escort Glenn and Marybeth down to the station. Their fate would be held with the judge and jury.

Jerry asked Dave what would happen next. "It depends if they have the money to be released on bail. They may go to prison or pay a hefty fine or both. Chances are, they'll get out within a few months anyway, but at least they won't have any dogs, any money, any shop—and hell, they might not even have a house."

"That's the happy ending I want to hear."

"Yeah," Peter said. "I just hope those dogs can be saved and adopted. Fifty is a big number."

"Sure is, Pete, but at least we aren't looking at fifty dead animals back there."

"You make a good point, Dave. Ha! Kyle is escorting Glenn to the police car. He must be loving life right now."

Kyle turned toward them and winked, as he accidentally-on-purpose bonked Glenn's head on the top of the car as he *assisted* him into the backseat.

Chapter 26: Foxy's Homecoming

One of the sweetest joys in life is watching a dog simply be a dog.

As promised, Anthony made good on his word to take the day off to celebrate Foxy's homecoming. Not only did he take the day, but he also went above and beyond for his new four-legged daughter.

As he pulled into a pet supply store, he playfully instructed his wife, "Wait here, honey."

Chelsea watched as he walked in, and she thought she must be imagining that he had a little more pep in his step.

As she waited patiently for her husband, she sat in the backseat of the truck with both Emma and Foxy. Emma slept and didn't feel a thing when Foxy gently licked her tiny fingers.

After fifteen minutes, Chelsea caught a glimpse of Anthony wheeling a large shopping cart toward the back of the truck. She was dumbfounded by the sheer quantity of items.

He lifted the hatch of the trunk, and she watched him load the items one by one: a purple dog bed, two small blankets, a large bag of rawhide bones, dog biscuits, four squeaky toys, seven or more stuffed animals—she lost count when she saw what else he had bought. There was a life vest for the pool, two books on training, and a hot-pink leash with matching collar—both with hearts on them.

Foxy's tail wagged as she watched.

When they got home, she ran up to the front door. They started to introduce her to the house, but found that they didn't need to. She remembered her surroundings.

Sugar and Spice greeted her with sniffs, whines, and drool, and the three took off from where they'd left off two years prior. While Chelsea thought Foxy might be subdued or intimidated, she adjusted without missing a beat. It was as if she'd never left. She even went to the crate where she used to sleep and crawled in to grab a toy without any hesitation. She was in an environment where there was nothing but trust. She had no reason to be fearful.

The three dogs romped around the backyard, each pummeling the other to the ground and initiating various other games of play for what seemed like hours on end.

As Anthony went to retrieve the life preserver for Foxy, Sugar and Spice jumped into the pool, and Foxy followed their lead—no life preserver needed. She swam after her biological parents and even smuggled the tennis ball out of Sugar's mouth.

Chelsea and Anthony watched, thoroughly moved by the pure innocence in which their dogs played, realizing what a difference they had made in the young dog's life. And realizing what a difference she had made in theirs.

There was nothing more right in the world.

Foxy was finally where she belonged.

Chapter 27: Two Weeks Later

If you have the ability to go the extra mile, do it. The small actions you take today can have a positive effect on many lives tomorrow.

Foxy had been adjusting quite well as she reunited with her long lost family, except for a small number of times that Chelsea caught her looking somewhat down in the dumps. After some thought, she surmised that it was due to the turmoil she'd experienced and the heartache of not seeing Nathan anymore.

It was on an early Monday morning when Chelsea received the call from Patricia. Nathan had been in the hospital for the entire two weeks. He had been making progress, and while the doctors did want to keep him admitted, they moved him down to a step-down unit in the children's ward for another two weeks to recover.

"Chelsea, I have great news! Well, let me rephrase that: I have decent news. It isn't the best, but they finally discovered what is wrong with Nathan. We switched doctors, and then they called in a specialist in pulmonary dysfunction."

"That's great, Patricia. What did they find?"

"Well, it's called obstructive sleep apnea. The specialist couldn't believe our first doctor didn't diagnose it or even suggest that it was a possibility. He also has asthma, but we already figured that. So, since he wasn't really getting a quality night's sleep, he became increasingly sluggish. The asthma compounded with the sleep apnea only added to his misery.

"Our first doctor did diagnose the asthma, but missed the telltale signs of this particular version of sleep apnea."

"Can it be treated?"

"Well, they performed surgery yesterday to remove his tonsils and adenoids. The specialist said this should improve his condition tremendously, and we need to help him use a positive airway pressure machine, which will prevent him from *not* breathing in his sleep."

"That's fantastic! At least now you know what it is and can do something about it." Chelsea was elated, but had to admit that a small, selfish part of her was paranoid that Patricia would ask her to return Foxy. Patricia proved her wrong before it even grew into a real concern.

"Oh, and I don't want you to worry. I'm only calling to share the good news. I'd never try to take Foxy back. It's clear to see she belongs to you. I'd love for Nathan just to see her when he's out, if that's all right with you."

Breathing a sigh of relief, Chelsea kicked herself for having the audacity to think such a thing. "Of course it's all right! I think it would be wonderful for Foxy as well, as she's been showing some minor signs of depression every now and again. That might be just the thing to lift her spirits. Since she's been through so much, I don't think there could ever be a wide enough circle of people that love her. Thanks so much for the phone call."

Before they hung up, Patricia let Chelsea know which hospital Nathan was in, as he'd be there for two more weeks for recovery and observation. Due to the severity of his previous ordeal, the doctors didn't want to leave any loose ends.

Chelsea hung up and pondered the situation for a few minutes. Much to her delight, she thought of the ideal way to cheer up both Nathan and Foxy.

Nothing like killing two birds with one stone.

Chapter 28: Amazing Findings

Some days, the answers might not jump out at you, but that doesn't mean you don't have the ability to find them. You just might not be looking in the right places.

On Tuesday morning, Chelsea sat down, sipped her coffee, and called the children's hospital where Nathan was recovering. With Sugar, Spice, and Foxy sitting obediently by her side, she asked the receptionist if the hospital allowed dogs on the premises.

The woman who answered the phone said that they did allow dogs every Wednesday, but they had to be certified therapy dogs, meaning they had to pass the Canine Therapy program (CTP).

At first Chelsea was discouraged, but then she pushed a little harder and asked a few more questions. "Well, what if they aren't a therapy dog?"

The woman answered bluntly, "Then they can't come in."

Every establishment has policies and regulations, but every so often those conventions can be bent just a hair. In this circumstance, Chelsea knew there had to be a slight exception to the rule. She just had to find it. "Not even for a minute? How about for a little boy who misses his dog?" Even though Foxy was no longer Nathan's dog, she figured a little white lie never hurt anyone. In Nathan's heart, Foxy was his dog.

The lady on the other end of the phone was a sucker for kids and dogs alike. At first, it didn't sound like she'd budge an inch, as Chelsea detected some attitude in her voice, but then her tone softened, and she remained quiet for a second.

"Well, if you were to come see this little boy, what time would you be arriving?"

She was finally getting somewhere. "I'd say around eleven."

"Eleven, huh? Listen, I don't normally do this and I could get into a lot of trouble, possibly even fired. But I can't resist being part of something that will make all the difference in a child's day. I can work something out for you. Come around to the back. There's a little picnic area for the children to go out and enjoy some fresh air. I'll meet you out there, but you can't stay long."

Chelsea thanked the woman up and down before hanging up. Normally she wouldn't be so assertive, but desperate times call for desperate measures. Chelsea was extremely grateful that this woman, who didn't know her from a hole in the wall, would be compassionate enough to make concessions to cheer up a child.

Chelsea knew Patricia would be with her son, so she figured she could surprise them both and bring Foxy along. Foxy's spirits would be lifted, so she'd certainly benefit from the visit as well.

Chelsea speculated that there were other underlying issues that contributed to Foxy's depression. She observed Foxy during some of those bouts of depression and noticed that, without fail, she sought comfort by grabbing her favorite toy in her mouth. She'd then coddle it and whimper, voicing desperation with each cry.

Unbeknownst to Chelsea, Foxy's behavior stemmed from when her pup had passed away and she had to watch Glenn scoop it up like it was nothing. For Foxy, this toy took the place of her baby.

Chelsea knew she had to work earnestly to help Foxy get back to a comfort zone, and she was more than prepared to do so. After all, it was Chelsea and Anthony who accidentally sold her to a puppy mill owner in the first place.

The next morning at eleven, Chelsea proceeded just as she'd planned. Emma's babysitter arrived at 10:45 as promised, while Chelsea took Foxy outside and helped her into the truck. Sugar and Spice watched protectively from the window as their pup left.

When they arrived at the children's hospital, they walked around back as instructed and saw Patricia sitting on a bench with Nathan and a nurse. The nurse was facing Chelsea, but Patricia and Nathan were sitting with their backs to the entrance. The nurse spotted Chelsea first and quietly motioned for her to come in.

As the gate clicked behind her, Nathan turned around and saw his best friend trot in. He shrieked out Foxy's name, only as he knew it. "Dixie!"

Patricia quietly corrected him. "Her name is now Foxy, honey."

He shrugged his shoulders as Foxy lavished him with puppy kisses all over his face. "I don't care. I like that name too." They all laughed at his unadulterated innocence as he bent down and smothered his old friend with giant hugs.

A few of the other children heard the commotion and promptly joined in the fun. Foxy thrived on the attention and wagged her tail vigorously. Other parents were notified that there would be a guest that day, and they were thrilled to see their children get such an emotional boost.

While the kids played with Foxy, the nurse approached Chelsea. She was a large woman of Spanish descent who spoke with a hint of an accent, mixing English and Spanish as she spoke. She had a wide, reassuring smile as she walked over to Chelsea. "*Hola*, you must be Chelsea. Nancy, the receptionist told me you were coming, so I brought a little entourage of children who haven't seen a dog in a while. I checked with their parents first, of course."

"Thanks so much. I didn't get your name."

"Ah, *sí. Mi nombre es* Marta."

"Thank you, Marta."

"No hay problema, but if we stay out here, I'm going to get into trouble. You can't stay long."

"I understand. We'll leave in a few minutes. Thank you so much for allowing this visit. Foxy has been through so much, and she and Nathan simply adore each other."

"It's my pleasure, but here's a thought. Why don't you register Foxy for a Canine Therapy Program evaluation? I'm sure she'll pass. Make her a therapy dog. She seems to enjoy being with people. You mentioned she's been through a lot. I heard it helps the dog just as much as the children."

"Really? Ya think so? Foxy was rescued from a puppy mill and is still adjusting. I wonder if that would help her."

"Oh, trust me, it'll be perfect. I had two of my dogs pass the test. They then became certified as therapy dogs. They were rescues too, and they love it. They no longer mope around; they're far from depressed. They now have a job to do, and it makes them feel important. Think about it."

"I will. Thank you so much!"

"*De nada.*"

Chelsea called Foxy over and bent down to give Nathan a hug good-bye. All the other children gave Foxy a dog-perfected high five before she left, and Foxy responded by wiggling her body and wagging her tail with unmistakable delight.

On the drive home, Chelsea pondered Marta's advice for a while before acknowledging that it might be exactly what Foxy needed.

She'd bring it up to her husband that night.

Chapter 29: Therapy

Hard work and perseverance—two of the most important ingredients for success.

Chelsea wanted to find creative new ways to approach Anthony with her latest ideas. Thankfully, he was an understanding and open-minded man, especially when it came to his wife.

Anthony listened carefully to Chelsea's pitch and, to her surprise, agreed wholeheartedly. He even offered to accompany her to the evaluation.

The Canine Therapy Program evaluation required that each dog be evaluated on a list of ten items. They need to pass each one to receive their certificate. Chelsea and Anthony retrieved that list of action items and worked earnestly on training Foxy for each one.

She mastered each of the items like a champ, except two: mingling with a stranger and being left in another's care while Chelsea left the room. After a month or so, she became so accustomed to mingling with a stranger that she welcomed the opportunity. She still wasn't thrilled when Chelsea left her alone, but she had definitely improved from when they first started training.

Chelsea worked with her between Emma's naps and then walked her and Emma at the same time to get Foxy acclimated to outside noises, people, and various everyday occurrences.

It was almost as if Foxy was obliterating the memories of her previous life and enjoying the present, even though Chelsea knew that she would never fully forget.

By six weeks after their visit with Marta, Foxy was ready to take her test. Anthony had been more involved and excited than Chelsea ever anticipated, wanting to be there every step of the way. They even got a babysitter for Emma while they brought Foxy in for evaluation.

As they waited in line, Foxy oozed confidence and wagged her tail at each person that walked by, greeting everyone with an abundance of fervor. It was a complete turnaround from when she was first captured.

When it was Foxy's turn, Chelsea had butterflies swarming in her stomach. She wanted so much for Foxy to have the best of everything, so she prayed that she would pass.

The evaluator performing the test didn't do much to ease the participants' minds. She was stiff as a board and had the lifeless personality to match. Her graying brown hair was tightly wrapped in a bun, and a whistle hung loosely around her neck. She was the last person Chelsea would've picked as a dog lover.

She acknowledged Chelsea with cold professionalism and Foxy much along the same lines.

Oh no, Foxy will never pass with this woman in charge, Chelsea thought, hoping she'd at least be nice to Foxy.

Foxy passed the first few exercise, with flying colors, proving Chelsea wrong. She greeted strangers with poise, remained in a "stay" position until called, and sat still while the evaluator knelt down and got eye level with her. For all nine items, she was perfect. When the tenth item was tested, Chelsea cringed, as she didn't think Foxy would make it. It was the dreaded test for separation anxiety. That was the one issue on the list that Foxy struggled with, typically whining when Chelsea left her in the hands of a stranger.

The evaluator took firm hold of the leash and instructed Chelsea to walk away. Anthony was to remain out of sight as well. As Chelsea turned her back, she heard the first whine. She thought, *Oh, Foxy, please be a good girl. I'll be right back, I promise.* Then another. Chelsea wanted to disappear to make it easier on Foxy, so she walked faster. She had to remain out of sight for three painstaking minutes.

Once the time was up, the evaluator called for Chelsea, who eagerly walked back with Anthony. She bit her lower lip as she waited to hear the results.

"Here's your dog, Mr. and Mrs. Shelton." The evaluator didn't even look them in the eyes as she handed them the handle. Chelsea knew that could only mean one thing. "Thank you," she said, as she took the leash and began walking away. All of that hard work for the past six weeks. All of the hope for Foxy to be a therapy dog thrown out the window. They praised Foxy anyway as they didn't want her to sense their disappointment

The evaluator called out to them. "Mr. and Mrs. Shelton? Don't you want this?" She was waving a piece of paper around like a fan, a slight grin on her face. She almost looked personable for a moment. "Here's Foxy's certificate. She passed. Congratulations!"

As Chelsea took the paper, the evaluator was already onto her next participant.

Anthony reached into his pocket for a large dog biscuit and slipped it to Foxy while they both commended her up and down. "Good girl! You're such a good girl, Foxy!" "Awooooo!" As they ruffled her fur, Foxy howled in agreement, sharing the excitement with her owners.

As expected, Anthony and Chelsea were intoxicated with exhilaration from Foxy's achievement. They believed wholeheartedly that when Foxy became a therapy dog, she'd regain the confidence that she once possessed and understand that she had a purpose in life.

The next Wednesday, Chelsea got Foxy ready and hung her credentials around her neck as they walked into the children's hospital. The receptionist who had initially bent the rules for them smiled warmly as she greeted them. Chelsea thanked her for allowing them to come. Marta met them in the hallway and escorted them to the wing where all of the children were waiting.

Inside, Chelsea was unsure of what to expect. Nathan had been released, so she'd be visiting with other children. Since this was her first time introducing Foxy as a certified therapy dog, the nurses briefed her about the children's' conditions. Some were merely recovering from minor surgeries, but others were in there for far more serious illnesses, such as leukemia and other forms of cancer. Seeing all of those innocent children in one room was a heart-wrenching experience for Chelsea. She couldn't even begin to fathom their strength and courage.

At such a young age, when children should only be worrying about which flavor of ice pop to have, many of them had already endured countless surgeries, dealing with pain, losing their hair, and sleepless nights.

Yet they all managed to share a smile. When they saw Foxy enter, that smile broadened, and the cares of the world fell by the wayside for a few precious moments. The children's eyes lit up when she walked by, and they giggled when her fluffy tail brushed their faces. Foxy walked in with confidence, as if she knew she had a very important job to do—chest out, chin up, and tail high and swinging like a pendulum.

Nathan and Patricia met Chelsea and Foxy at the hospital, as Nathan wanted to see all the friends he had made during his stay. He was proud as could be when he boasted that Foxy was his stepsister; the rest of the kids cheered.

From that day forward, Chelsea went back every Wednesday to visit the children. The happiness it brought both them and Foxy was worth every moment. It got to the point where Foxy proudly retrieved her own special collar with her earned credentials and brought it to Chelsea for assistance in putting it on.

Foxy's confidence showed marked improvement with each week that passed. No longer was she scared of strange noises and no longer did she fear staying outside by herself; she knew her new owner would always let her back in.

Chapter 30: No Longer Forgotten

Rescues. Though they may not have voices to thank you for saving their lives, it is guaranteed that they do.

Patricia and Chelsea became fast friends, and Nathan acted as an older brother to Emma whenever they came by to visit. Lori also had a special place in her heart for Foxy, so she came by frequently, as did Braden and Melissa.

Both families were concerned about the other dogs that were rescued from the mill and kept in contact with their veterinarians, Dr. Fredericks and Dr. Hill.

They were saddened to learn that three of the dogs didn't make it, as their wounds and infections had been too severe. The humane thing to do was to euthanize them, as their life would have been reduced to endless pain and suffering. So, out of a recovery of fifty-two dogs from the mill and nine puppies from the store—a total of sixty-one—the veterinarians and their team were able to save fifty-eight.

The animals were given to no-kill animal rescue groups throughout the valley and local news teams advertised the story for free. An influx of calls came in to the centers from families looking to adopt. Of course, due to the sensitive nature of the dogs' previous lives, a thorough screening was given to ensure that history wouldn't repeat itself.

To further prevent a replication of past events, all of the dogs and puppies were neutered or spayed. A third of them were adopted or were in the process of being adopted, while others were still in recovery. There were people on waiting lists who promised to adopt once the dogs were healthy enough.

As for the remainder of the rescues, some were either dog aggressive or people aggressive, and local trainers worked with them for free to rehabilitate them. The hope was that they would then be considered adoptable.

And as soon as Nathan was given medical clearance, his family adopted two of the rescued dogs as well.

***

On the other side of town, in a dimly lit brick building sat Glenn and Marybeth Kennedy in cells separated by gender. They were caged in steel bars, much like the environment in which their dogs had suffered.

Since they had lived without honor or integrity, they had no one to stand up for them and bail them out. Their house fell into foreclosure, their shop was closed, and their bank accounts were drained bone dry.

In addition to the charges filed against them from their shady business practices were other charges Kyle hadn't even discovered. It was safe to say that they would be living the same lifestyle their dogs had once endured. Karma had caught up with them and delivered exactly what they deserved.

If and when they were released from prison, they would never be allowed to own a dog and wouldn't even have the financial means to do so. The macabre hole that they dug was a deep one and was devouring them.

Justice had finally prevailed, and Glenn and Marybeth would never be able to do something so dreadfully awful ever again.

Epilogue: Justice Prevails

For those dogs that are born free but tossed into a life of confinement through no fault of their own, there are thousands who ache to see them running through the sand free and joyful. The small action of one positive thought can snowball into greater things and have an astounding influence on the future.

Since they lived in the desert, Sugar, Spice, and Foxy never experienced the joys of the beach. Noticing how they all enjoyed swimming in their built-in pool, Chelsea and Anthony wanted to reward them with more. They deserved a little vacation. So they planned a weekend for their treasured dogs and drove down to San Diego.

Sugar, Spice, and Foxy leapt out of the car at the beach and waited for the one command: "Go play!" They ran toward the water in a race to see who could get there first, leaving three sets of paw prints in the sand—clearly signifying the epitome of freedom and pleasure.

Watching the three of the dogs united as a family, splashing around in the water, confirmed their decision—one they had made when they walked into that shelter years ago.

After meeting Jerry and his clan through Dr. Hill's and Dr. Frederick's introductions, they talked with them about opening a no-kill shelter. Fortunately, money wasn't a problem for any of them, and Chelsea had stopped working since Emma was born, so she had time on her hands.

Jerry, Dave, Kyle, and Pete agreed to volunteer two days each week, rearranging their full-time jobs so that the shelter would never be without someone to feed the dogs and give them ample time to exercise. Patricia, Lori, and

Braden all offered to volunteer as well. Even Melissa agreed to come by after school a few days a week.

So Chelsea could work at the shelter, the team blueprinted a secure playroom just for Emma, which would be transformed into an extra room for the dogs when Emma got older. Anthony was more than happy to devote his free time to saving homeless animals as well.

So much happiness had been granted to them when they adopted Sugar and Spice and then rescued Foxy. They wanted nothing more than to help as many homeless animals as they could.

***

As she watched their dogs run carefree at the beach, Chelsea thought of the perfect name for the shelter. When she got back into town, she set up a meeting to discuss it with the group. They all agreed and loved it.

When they began construction on the building, the first thing created was a wood-burned plaque of Foxy, the inspiration behind it all and then, the sign: Paw Prints in the Sand.

Simply because there's nothing in the world like watching a dog frolic through sand and surf with nothing but pure joy and exhilaration.

And at no time should any dog be confined to life in a cage.

Ever.

Note from the Author:

Although this book and the groups/organizations in this book are a work of fiction and a complete figment of my imagination, unfortunately puppy mills and backyard breeders are quite real. The fears and quirks I've described in this book are extremely common with rescue dogs.

The environment for puppy mill dogs is incomprehensible. Keep in mind that while not all, many puppy stores do get their puppies from puppy mills and it is a continuing practice here in the United States.

There are plenty of shelters or animal rescue groups from which to adopt, or if you are seeking a specific breed, find a reputable breeder. You should be able to get the dog's paperwork without any issues. If there is an issue, that might be an indication that the puppy is from a puppy mill.

In addition, many puppy stores will state that you can *exchange* your puppy for another one if the one you bought is sick. Please note, that the puppy you then return will most likely be euthanized because it is too much of a financial liability to get the medical attention that it desperately needs.

Again, not all puppy stores operate in this fashion, but it would be worth it to do your research before you make purchase.

Additionally, if a pedigree puppy is what you desire, many animal shelters and animal rescue groups DO have pedigrees and often, they are puppies. You might be surprised at how many purebred puppies are given up to an animal rescue group.

If that doesn't have you convinced, perhaps this will. Speaking from experience, there is no greater reward than rescuing a pet. They are perfect companions and stick by you through thick and thin.

You'll enjoy their appreciation, love and loyalty for their entire precious life.

Thanks for reading!

ALSO WRITTEN BY ELIZABETH PARKER:
Paw Prints in the Sand:
Mission Accomplished

Sequel to "Paw Prints in the Sand"

The game of life. It's a challenging one-- sometimes breeding days of triumph while other times propagating feelings of despair.

Many have found a way to enjoy a balance-- counting their blessings when times are good and finding comfort with loved ones when the cards are stacked against them.

Others are not as fortunate, taking life's trials to heart, letting them fester into the very depths of their soul, allowing tragedy to dig seemingly irreparable trenches in their hearts.

What they may not realize is that there is a way to tunnel themselves out and patch those dark holes. The picture they've painted for themselves might appear dismal and bleak, but if they make the choice to paint with a different brush, they have the power to change their outlook--quite often with a little help.

You often hear stories about how people rescue dogs, but quite often, it is the opposite that is true. For Harrison Carter, his canvas couldn't have displayed a more dreadful future, but that was about to turn around for him. He was about to discover one of the best kept secrets for happiness. One he never thought could...and would change his life forever. It just so happened that it involved a four-legged creature with a furry coat and a fluffy tail.

A Fictional Novella.

*A portion of the proceeds will be donated to animal rescue.

Finally Home

"There is a time in everyone's life where they have been emotionally inspired or amazed by something that was completely unexpected. Sometimes it is so touching, that they want to share their experience with the world and tell their story.

This particular story is about a precious heart along with a free-spirited little boy who owns that heart. This little boy has expressive brown eyes, a beautiful smile, and golden brown coat that he never takes off. He also has a huge pinkish-brown nose and four very fast legs. His name is Buddy. He answers to that...when he wants to."

Buddy was a dog that no one wanted, yet he became one of the quirkiest, friendliest, smartest and most cherished of dogs. The reader is not only drawn into the book, but learns from the unfortunate mistakes of others and how to think outside of the proverbial box. It gives the reader hope that if they are going through a similar ordeal, they can also successfully overcome any related obstacle.

If you are looking for a great gift for both dog lovers and even non-dog lovers, this book is perfect. Get ready to laugh a little and perhaps even shed a few tears.

A portion of the proceeds from the sale of "Finally Home" will be donated to an animal rescue group.

Final Journey: Buddys' Book

After the publication of "Finally Home," Buddy was diagnosed with terminal cancer. Once the unthinkable happened and Buddy's precious life was cut short, his family was left heartbroken and devastated.

At the same time, in another state, poor economic conditions forced another family to give up their golden retriever.

As fate would have it, his name...was Buddy.

While they were mourning the loss of their beloved dog, another dog was mourning the loss of his treasured family.

Brought together by misfortune, they entered each other's lives to help put back together the pieces of their broken hearts.

This story is for both Buddys, producing the subtitle "Buddys' Book."

*A portion of the proceeds from the sale of this book will be donated to an animal rescue organization.

Phobia

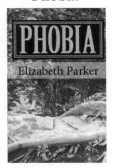

Growing up with phobias that have terrified him his entire life, Matt Brewer had finally made the decision to go to counseling, seeking help once and for all.

He entrusted his emotions in the hands of strangers and depended on them to help conquer his fear. What he did not count on was having his fears become a distinct reality, leaving him fighting for his life and the lives of those around him, including his girlfriend whom he intended to marry.

Tortured and bound, he comes face to face with evil with no one to hear his screams. Time is of the essence and it's a literal race against the clock in order to make it out alive.

*A portion of the proceeds from the sale of this book will be donated to a dog rescue organization.

Unwanted Dreams

What if the life you were living was not the one you were meant to live?

One man. One moment in time. One horrific night. That was all it took.

Alexandra had married the man of her dreams and they had their whole life ahead of them. They had a wonderful marriage, a beautiful house and essentially they could not be happier. Things were falling into place as intended, until one beautiful evening turned devastatingly tragic.

The catastrophic events that transpired ensured that none of their lives would ever be the same. Faced with an impossible moral decision, Alex had to make a choice that would come back to haunt her in years to come, once again forcing her to tempt the hands of fate.

How does a random murder shatter the many lives of those within the killer's path? How do you pick up the pieces of your life when unforeseen circumstances alter your future forever?

Unwanted Dreams provides just the right amount of twists and turns, leaving the reader in suspense, pondering the following question: How strong is the bond that exists between families and how far would you be willing to go to save your own?

*A portion of the proceeds from the sale of this book will be donated to a dog rescue organization.

Evil's Door

Childhood rumors are often prevalent in a family-oriented community. Some boast that they have seen a UFO flying overhead while others claim to have witnessed a ghost soaring through the trees. Some stories are so believable that they trickle down from sibling to sibling, friend to friend; creating a neighborhood buzz that lingers for years.

Ryan Sheffield's neighborhood was no different. Though no one would admit it, adults and children alike were freaked out by the eccentric woman who lived in the ghastly corner house, but aside from that, his world as he knew it was an ordinary one.

Bizarre situations did not surface until Ryan began working at his very first job. To his peers and superiors, it was just a traditional office. To Ryan, it was much more than that after a series of inexplicable occurrences haunted his every conscious moment.

Through a bit of intense research, he uncovered the building's gruesome history and was led down its horrifying path. He opened the door to a hell he did not want to live in and tried his best to avoid the evil that surrounded him. The truth revealed itself to him in more ways than one; a truth he was better off not knowing and one that could essentially end his life.

*A portion of the proceeds from the sale of this book will be donated to an animal rescue organization.

Bark Out Loud!

"Bark Out Loud" is a compilation of motivational and thought-provoking quotes—some about dogs and some about life in general—that have been inspired by my own dogs, as well as those that I've met and those that I'll never have the opportunity to meet. Many of the quotes are meant to motivate, some are meant to initiate a smile and others are simply thoughts to ponder. All of the animal-related pictures in this book are either of dogs or cats that we—or someone we know— had the opportunity to rescue. If you enjoy goofy photographs of animals or pretty landscape pictures along with uplifting words, then this book is for you!

A portion of the proceeds will be donated to animal rescue organizations.

*Please note this is a short book under fifty pages.

My Dog Does That!

Are you a dog-lover? If so, you're not alone!

My Dog Does That! is a humorous, uplifting, feel-good book about what all dog-lovers have in common: dogs and the reasons that we love them.

Some days they make us laugh, other days they make us crazy, but one thing is for certain; they do some interesting things that non dog-lovers wouldn't understand.

Do you ever feel a bit awkward due to the stunts that your dog has pulled? Do you ever feel as if you are the only one whose dog embarrasses them at not-so-convenient times? How about those wonderfully sweet and tender moments that you so badly want to brag about, but are afraid others may not understand?

We dog-lovers can all relate to the everyday occurrences when it comes to our furry friends because our dogs do that too!

Faces of Deception

Jacqueline was invincible. As a young teen, she knew what she wanted and how to achieve it. Even when she was framed and arrested for a crime she didn't commit, she managed to pick up the pieces of her life and move forward.

In a world apart from hers, Montgomery Vendora carved himself a life full of crime, deceiving those closest to him and taking chances without regret. There would be no reason for their lives to ever collide.

When a series of unfortunate incidents find their place in her life, including accidentally stumbling upon incriminating key evidence, Jacqueline's world begins to crumble. She is forced to avenge fate, playing a role she had never intended to take part in, receiving help from an unexpected source.

Made in the USA
Middletown, DE
30 August 2023